Monique
ha-Buth
Hart

The Uses of Disorder

By Richard Sennett
in Norton Paperback

The Conscience of the Eye:
The Design and Social Life of Cities

The Fall of Public Man

The Uses of Disorder:
Personal Identity and City Life

RICHARD SENNETT

The
USES
of
DISORDER:

Personal Identity & City Life

W. W. Norton

New York · London

First published as a Norton paperback 1992 by
arrangement with Alfred A. Knopf, Inc.

Library of Congress Catalog Card Number: 71–106628

ISBN 0–393–30909–6

W. W. Norton & Company, Inc.
500 Fifth Avenue, New York, N.Y. 10110
W. W. Norton & Company Ltd
10 Coptic Street, London WC1A 1PU

Printed in the United States of America

2 3 4 5 6 7 8 9 0

For Carol

Acknowledgments

The idea for this book came to me during a walk with Erik Erikson one morning in a New England graveyard. I should like to thank him for the steady encouragement he gave me in subsequent months. I should also like to thank Jon Cobb, Jane White, and my wife, Carol, for helping me find the intellectual direction of my reflections. I owe a special debt of thanks to Angus Cameron, who helped me define the purpose of this book at a critical stage of the writing.

Contents

Introduction

During the past decade people of diverse social backgrounds and political opinions have awakened to the need to reconstruct city life. The riots forced mass attention on black poverty, but young people, who came alive in the 1960's after the silence of the previous generation, have developed an interest in cities that is more wide-ranging. For they have sensed in dense city life some possibility of fraternity, some new kind of warmth, that is now understood in the vague term "community."

In large part, the search of young people outside the ghetto for urban community of this sort, for a relatedness and sharing, has been self-defeating. Some people tried to find this relatedness in the black ghetto itself, but the solidarity of the black brothers was bought at the expense of much pain and is not for outside consumption. The blacks told the affluent whites to find the warmth in themselves. Some people tried to find community by radicalizing the working class, but the working class is not buying a student alliance these days and broke kids' heads when it responded to them at all.

So the search for community has come to be a search for some life principle in young people as they are— white, affluent, and unhappy with the cocoons their parents spun around them. And the process of elimination that has forced this search back to an honest self-analysis has also brought the movement for social and personal renewal to a standstill. What does it mean for a white, educated, affluent person to feel a sense of community with other people? People in the suburbs have a sense of togetherness, of possessing an identity, a sense of "we" as a community, but that kind of social cohesion is exactly what most people nurtured in suburbs are seeking to escape. It is freedom of some kind that is included in this vague new ideal of community, but what kind of community freedom is there beyond the freedom from material want?

Here is obviously no small problem, no little twist in our history. This is the first generation that has lived with both the achievement of affluence *(wealth)* as a constant force in life, and the problems of what to do with it. Yet the force of change released in the last decade has come to an impasse precisely because this generation has none of the old hiding places left, cannot pretend to identify itself as a voice of the blacks or the white poor. It is left with the real problem of making a social life out of its own social materials, out of affluence and freedom from the struggle against scarcity and want. And it has no model from the generation that brought the affluence into being, since the willful innocence of the suburbs does not seem to be a satisfying way to sustain a social life, seems in fact to be a voluntary servitude to unruffled ease.

If and when the United States ends its venture in Vietnam, if people can draw the lesson and end the morass of endless military expenditure, there will be an enormous amount of funds that can, and perhaps economically must, be spent on domestic renewal. The "generation gap" will then be posed anew. If we want to end the physical depravity of slum housing, slum education, slum health, what should we do: build as we have before, and so induct the blacks and the poor whites into the malaise already felt by the white children of affluence? Increasingly, the poor are voicing their objections to that old way; they are saying that the ghetto brownstones are better, in the end, than the marvels of the new housing projects; something essential, also called "community," is eclipsed by entry into the city forms of affluence as things now stand.

Affluence Across the Revolutionary Line

One of the strangest features of modern community life is that this problem has crossed the revolutionary line. The post-Revolutionary order in Russia and in its more affluent satellites seems exposed to a complex of dangers that were supposed to be stilled in the process of revolutionary upheaval. The young in these countries see their parents using affluence in ways they find disturbing; a kind of willful simplicity in the families of bureaucrats and a routinization of the pattern of daily life seem as deadening to young people in Moscow as they do to young people in New York. Again the problem: What does one do with community life when freedom from want has been achieved? The Revolution redistributed wealth, but the fact of Revolution did not determine how the eventual affluence was to be taken into a life, what men would dedicate themselves to when they no longer needed to struggle for enough to eat.

Many revolutionary writers have expressed concern about what their societies have to sustain beyond the fact of the old injuries. Their thoughts, like those of young people in our society, have come to focus on what kind of community sharing ought to reign under conditions of relative economic plenitude. Men like Herbert Marcuse and Franz Fanon have arrived at a specific answer. They believe that the revolutionary passage ought to be an emotional experience that transcends ridding a society of tyrants; it should be an education accustoming men to accept a certain amount of anarchy and disorder in their lives. To change the leaders of a society without changing the amount of disorder that the society will bear is ultimately to have no revolution at all. Marx, in his manuscripts of 1844, understood this; to be free in a post-revolutionary world was, he wrote, to transcend the need for order. Yet in Marx's early work was the dream that economic abundance would itself remove the structural need in society for order. At that time he believed that repressive order grew not merely out of the inequitable distribution of wealth but also out of the fact that there was not enough to go around. This is why critics like Sartre see in Marx the philosopher of plenitude, of a society that could exist beyond the order produced by economic scarcity.

Of the revolutionary writers who saw that this dream of freedom would not arise from the brute fact of redistribution, Franz Fanon, the Algerian psychiatrist, has been the most explicit in spelling out what kind of community structure is necessary in the post-revolutionary society to achieve the goal of nonroutine life. For Fanon, the freedom inherent in making revolution can only live as long as the revolutionaries remain outside the confines of city life; he believed they must look at the city as a human settlement, a human community, hostile to the force of their own commitment. Fanon believed that the necessity for bureaucracy in a city and the anonymous character of human contacts there were bound, in the end, to destroy the feeling of closeness, of men wanting to share a better, more just life for all. By the same token, these dense places would frighten men into pursuing safe routines where they knew they would not be overwhelmed. They would thus be pushed into private circles of security and eventually lost as revolutionaries.

This anti-urban bias of revolutionary leaders who are disturbed by what has transpired in Russia is deep-seated; it is to be seen in the glorification of the peasantry by Mao Tse-tung and Fidel Castro; it is to be seen in the theorists of guerrilla warfare who are increasingly giving up the cities as "hopeless" places in which to inflame widespread revolutionary ideals.

But the fear of cities displayed by men like Fanon leads itself to a terrible limit on human freedom. Avoiding city life may preserve the ardor of solidarity, but at the cost of enforcing a terrible simplicity, that of the tribe or small village, on the revolutionaries. The price of keeping the revolutionary spirit alive is thus a bondage of its own, a curb on the social diversity present when many different people live together in a dense, urban settlement.

The urge to avoid routine is gratified, ironically, by making the social boundaries of life claustrophobic.

Furthermore, the problems of large-scale organization are ignored rather than confronted. Better tribal and intimate than impersonal and bureaucratic is a formula whose exercise is an admission of impotence to deal with and change bureaucratic structures of themselves. Thus do the theories of the anti-urban revolutionaries come against the same problem now facing the New Left in Western countries: How can the urban-based large-scale bureaucracies be transformed so that better communal lives are possible? It is a question of learning how to use the system of life-producing affluence in order not to be smothered by it.

I think men like Marcuse and Fanon are right when they say there is a need to learn a new context of disorder and diversity; the rules and routines necessary to survive in the face of economic scarcity are now out of place. But I have been moved in my own thinking to probe how dense, disorderly, overwhelming cities can become the tools to teach men to live with this new freedom.

I have had to start with the premise the history of the postwar years taught this generation: communities of abundance open up new possibilities in men for self-imposed tyranny as well as for freedom. To understand the community life of people freed from scarcity requires a sounding of the darker desires of men, desires for safe and secure slavery that people bring into their social relations. Only by probing feelings of this sort, which most men would be loathe to admit to themselves, can come clear the quality of desiring freedom and the means of achieving it under conditions of modern affluence.

Unlike writers such as Erich Fromm and Hannah Arendt, who treat the desire for slavery on a broad psychological palette, I have come to believe that this desire, as related to economically abundant community life, has a quite specific form: the line between slavery and freedom in rich communities depends on the character of the transition it is possible for men to make from adolescence to adulthood. The theme of this book is that there appears in adolescence a set of strengths and desires which can lead in themselves to a self-imposed slavery; that the current organization of city communities encourages men to enslave themselves in adolescent ways; that it is possible to break through this framework to achieve an adulthood whose freedom lies in its acceptance of disorder and painful dislocation; that the passage from adolescence to this new, possible adulthood depends on a structure of experience that can only take place in a dense, uncontrollable human settlement—in other words, in a city. The book aims to convince its readers of something distasteful now to most: the jungle of the city, its vastness and loneliness, has a positive human value. Indeed, I think certain kinds of disorder need to be increased in city life, so that men can pass into a full adulthood and so that, as I hope to show, men will lose their current taste for innocent violence.

Conservative readers may at first feel comfortable with this idea, since it may appear that the ideas and discontents of the young can be dismissed as pernicious illusions, which will disappear when they grow up. But it is precisely because the structure of present affluent community life discounts the release of new strengths and passions in adolescence, as though an early stage of life were not as dignified as a later one, that these feelings cannot be fully expressed and worked through. Thus do these urges toward voluntary slavery remain present and unresolved. Adults in affluent communities are frozen in desires that emerged in their adolescence and that have led them to a fear of the full possibilities of freedom in adulthood. But in the structure of a great city, men can be offered the possibility to move out of this morass; it is in the building of purposely diverse cities that society can provide men the experience of breaking from self-slavery to freedom as adults.

I believe the freedom to accept and to live in disorder represents the goal which this generation has aimed for, vaguely and inchoately, in its search for "community." The attempt I have made to refine and deepen the terms of the search for community is itself too vague and inchoate, I fear, to be a "proof" or a grand theory. I felt the need to question my own conscience, and hope you, the reader, will be moved to do the same.

PART ONE

A New Puritanism

CHAPTER ONE

Purified Identity

IN 1929 ANDRÉ MALRAUX PUBLISHED HIS FIRST NOVEL,
The Conquerors, a story of the leaders of the Chinese
Revolution of 1925. Malraux's American publisher has
written of this book, "It was indeed the first modern novel
in which the raw material of politics was subordinated
to the real subject matter: the characters' search for the
meaning of their lives." The real subject matter was what
we would now call the psychology of their struggle, the
passions leading them to revolution.

At the center of this novel lies a clash between two
kinds of leaders. Borodin and Garine are Russian revolutionaries in China guiding the native revolutionary cadres;
Hong is a young Chinese who is an anarchist, originally
part of the Borodin-Garine groups, but who later comes
into bitter conflict with them.

Borodin and Garine are Marxist revolutionaries, but
they are not ideologues. The struggle they are waging is in
terms of concrete events and specific people, so that their
philosophies of right bend, and are transformed by, the

specific processes of revolution they experience. Borodin and Garine are not merely "tacticians"; they fight for a reason, for a cause, but that cause is not impervious to the unique, unclassifiable events the revolution spawns.

Hong, their eventual enemy, is an anarchist, yet curiously much more rigid than they are. His sense of what is the right thing to do, what is "correct," flies in the face of the facts of the revolution; Hong is unwilling to bend, he cannot submit himself to the chaos of events in order to act, he cannot yield himself and his commitment to the test of conflicting experiences in the actual struggle. Instead, Hong must put himself in such a position that he seems to stand above the chaos, to be safe while the others are troubled, to be willfully immune when Garine and Borodin have the courage to be self-doubting and confused.

Certainly the drama Malraux fashioned out of these men's lives—a drama based on real persons—comes from their exceptional strengths at a special historic moment. Yet what makes these revolutionaries worth exploring is not simply their distinctiveness. Malraux distilled into the character of a man like Hong the essence of certain motives for action that guide less exceptional, weaker men in their everyday affairs. It is this hidden affinity with the routine world that makes Hong so startling and the forces animating him so important.

The feelings of young doctors about to start their careers as psychiatrists seem as distant in tone and temper from the emotions of revolutionary leaders battling in China as can be imagined. Therefore it might be worth-

4

while to look at ways the two groups of men can be guided by a common set of desires.

Recently two American researchers, Daniel Levenson and Myron Sharaf, did a study of a peculiar phenomenon among these young doctors. This was the tendency shown by many beginning psychiatrists to think of themselves as little gods, sitting in judgment on their patients and slightly contemptuous of them. The attitude, which Levenson and Sharaf called the psychiatrists' omnipotence desire, is of course not universal, but it is frequently to be found among newly practicing therapists.

In the process of their research Levenson and Sharaf concluded that this little-god complex occurred partially out of a great fear these new practitioners had that they might be hurt by becoming involved with the problems of their patients, involved in a painful way so deeply that their own sense of themselves would dissolve. The attitude of sitting in judgment from afar, with its hidden trace of contempt, was how these new doctors defended themselves from this fear, drew a line in advance for themselves as to who they were and the relation in which they stood to their patients.

Both Hong, the young revolutionary, and these young doctors have exerted a peculiar kind of strength—a power to cut themselves off from the world around them, to make themselves distant, and perhaps lonely, by defining themselves in a rigid way. This fixed self-definition gives them a strong weapon against the outside world. They prevent a pliant traffic between themselves and men around them and so acquire a certain immunity to the

pain of conflicting and tangled events that might otherwise confuse and perhaps even overwhelm them. In
Hong, this defense against confusion through a rigid
self-image is used to fend off the dissonance spawned by
revolutionary upheaval. By making himself immutably
fixed in purpose and act, Hong can transcend the experiences of horror, of guilt over killing, of sheer nerve-wrack-
ing tension that his comrades feel in their battles with
the police and the city populace. In the young doctors,
this defense against confusion through a rigid self-image
fends off being engulfed by the enormity of their patients'
pain, a pain whose sickness lies in part in the very fact that
the patients have no way to control it. For both the revolutionary and the doctors, the threat of being overwhelmed
by difficult social interactions is dealt with by fixing a
self-image *in advance,* by making oneself a fixed object
rather than an open person liable to be touched by a
social situation.

The sense of time involved in these acts of self-defense
is more complicated than it might first appear. A peculiar
behavior pattern among certain city planners, seemingly
remote from either of these two situations, shows what
this complexity is.

One technique of planning large human settlements
developed in the past hundred years has been the device
of establishing "projective needs." This means guessing
the future physical and social requirements of a community or city and then basing present spending and
energy so as to achieve a readiness for the projected
future state. In planning schools, beginning students
usually argue that people's lives in time are wandering

and unpredictable, that societies have a history in the sense that they do what was not expected of them; so that this device is misleading. Planning teachers usually reply that of course the projected need would be altered by practical objections in the course of being worked out; the projective-need analysis is a pattern of ideal conditions rather than a fixed prescription.

But the facts of planning in the last few years have shown that this disclaimer on the part of planners is something they do not really mean. Professional planners of highways, of redevelopment housing, of inner-city renewal projects have treated challenges from displaced communities or community groups as a threat to the value of their plans rather than as a natural part of the effort at social reconstruction. Over and over again one can hear in planning circles a fear expressed when the human beings affected by planning changes become even slightly interested in the remedies proposed for their lives. "Interference," "blocking," an "interruption of work" —these are the terms by which social challenges or divergences from the planners' projections are interpreted. What has really happened is that the planners have wanted to take the plan, the projection in advance, as more "true" than the historical turns, the unforeseen movements in the real time of human lives.

Why planners should be so inclined to think this way is a subject to be explored in detail later in this book. But the elements of their feelings can be discerned through what has been seen so far. City planning of this sort is the projection of a rigid group self-image similar in its motivation to the rigid individual self-images seen in the young revolutionary and in the group of young psychiatrists. For in this projected future there lies a way of denying the dissonance and unexpected conflicts of a society's history. This attitude is a means of denying the idea of history, i.e., that a society will come to be different than it expected to be in the past. In this way, a planner at his desk can steel himself against the unknown outside world in the same way that a young doctor steels himself against his fear about the experience of dealing with his patients by playing the little god, distant and removed. For this mechanism of defense to work, then, there is a necessity for a certain kind of millennial thinking, a fear of the sources of human diversity that create history in its true sense.

When this fearful defense against the unknown future becomes regnant in a life, the acceptable future can be conceived only in the same form as the present, as a state of life for an individual or group whose features are rigidly determined and contain no hidden surprises.

Norman Cohn's brilliant book, *The Pursuit of the Millennium,* investigated the lives of those unusual people and cults in the medieval era whose sense of time was governed in this way. His book concludes with a bold essay linking the sources of modern millenarian movements, like the Nazis in Germany, to these patterns of the past. But I think the people Cohn studies are examples of a human phenomenon even more general than Cohn takes them to be. These millenarians have played out in a striking way an endemic pattern of human fear, whose traces can be found in the attitudes of such seemingly "rationalistic" people today as young doctors or city engineers, or in such anti-religious leaders as the anarchist Malraux described.

However, the model for what this pattern of fear and self-conception means does come most easily from religion. The process described thus far can be called a search for purity. The effect of this defensive pattern is to create in people a desire for a purification of the terms in which they see themselves in relation to others. The enterprise involved is an attempt to build an image or identity that coheres, is unified, and filters out threats in social experience. Naturally the drives for purification of the self that occur in deeply religious people cannot be "reduced" or simplified so that they are explained simply as a fear of the unknown. But, socially, fear of losing one's identity through outside threats often does play a large element in religious conversions. Michael Walzer's account of the sources of cohesion in the original Puritan community, for example, shows how the turmoil of social change and an unknown future produced among the Puritans a great fear of not knowing who they were. This fear in turn produced in their religious affairs the desire to find an absolute identity, to be fully and finally known to each other as true believers.

The search for purity in more modern, less religious, terms is for someone like the anarchist Hong the desire to create so clear and unambiguous a self-image that he becomes immune to the outside world. The jarring elements in one's social life can be purified out as unreal because they don't fit that articulated object, that self-consciously spelled-out set of beliefs, likes and dislikes, and abilities that one takes to be oneself. In this way, the degree to which people feel urged to keep articulating who they are, what they want, and what they feel is almost an index of their fear about their inability to survive in social experience with other men.

The seekers after purity in more religious times seemed revolutionaries to the men around them. The Puritans, or the millenarians of an even earlier era, were impatient with the ills of the temporal world and acted to make it over—or at least the swatches of it they controlled—in their own image. Indeed, today one of the easy clichés about some young revolutionaries is that their desire for purity in the society and in themselves creates the revolutionary drive.

But hidden in this desire to purify one's identity to others and oneself is a conservative tendency. The known in this scheme of identity is so insistently taken as true that new unknowns which don't fit are excluded. Reality cannot be permitted to be other than what is encompassed in one's clearly articulated images of oneself and one's world. The obvious result, then, is that the material for change, change in one's feelings, one's beliefs, one's desires, is greatly weakened in a life because new events or experiences are being measured in terms of how well they correspond to a pre-existent pattern. The advent of unexpected experience is not permitted a reality of its own; the fear involved in the identity process prohibits men from feeling themselves free historical beings. Thus does this passion to create a clear self-identity act to conserve the known past in the face of the disturbing present. The historical turn, the event or experience that doesn't fit preconceived feelings and one's sense of place, is deflated in its "truth value." Because of this fear, the more comfortable, the easier dicta of the past are made the final standard of reference.

The attitudes of the young revolutionary, the young doctors, and the planners are thus bound together by one truly reactionary force: experience over the course of time is subjected to a purification process, so that the threatening or painful dissonances are warded off to preserve intact a clear and articulated image of oneself and one's place in the world. Experience is being purified by having the dissonances interpreted as less real than the consonances with what is known.

This, in crude outline, is how I believe the desire for purity can dominate the acts of people no longer enmeshed in the substantive problems of religion. Social-psychological thinking in the past decades has tried to understand ideas such as this in what are called "life-cycle," or developmental, terms. This approach is unlike that of the pioneer social-psychological thinkers. Freud, for example, treated the psychic processes of men as all in germ at the moment of birth; the instinctualists working on physiological problems believed set instincts innate to the organism played themselves out in changing recombination over the course of a lifetime. The newer social-psychological thinking is typified in psychoanalysis by men like Erik Erikson and pervades such movements of thought in the last twenty years as existential psychotherapy. These newer schools attempt to see how psychic materials, not just psychological problems, are generated during the course of a human lifetime; they are searching for ways to find how men create their psychologies. The new wave of psychological thinking rejects the idea that men are assigned their motives by such abstractions as "human nature" or "innate drives."

I believe that the peculiar desire for purity I have sketched so far is an emotion *created* at a specific point in men's lives. Of course it is true that human beings of all ages, from the infant to the old man about to die, have fears about the unknown. But it is no less true that the way human beings want to deal with fears and the powers men have to deal with them change radically *in kind* over the course of a lifetime. The peculiar response to fear of the unknown that leads to this search for a purification of one's relations with the social world is inaugurated, I believe, in adolescence. To understand this modern purity ritual, it is necessary to know something about the way the late-adolescent stage of life creates devices to handle disorder or painful threats.

– *The Emergence of Purified Identity*

Were one to follow the wisdom of the contemporary press, the group of adolescents who would seem under the sway of this need for a rigid identity would be the young in revolt. Yet the young people whom the press labels as student leaders are actually deviants from the real body of student unrest. These newspaper-created "student rebels" are ideologues, whose political ideas are a throwback to the primitive formulas of the 1930's.

A great body of the young are disaffected, to be sure, but their alienation is much more courageous, precisely because they have, in my experience, the integrity to be confused about what they want for themselves. Perhaps because these young people are trying to construct a decent life for themselves without the old, easy guides, the simplicity entailed in press reporting must ignore them. But in good studies, such as those by Jack Newfield or Kenneth Keniston, the reader can only be struck by how few are under the sway of the "new fascism," as the press calls it, or under the sway of Progressive Labor Party dogma. Rather, these affluent radicals are experimenters with themselves, and so are willing to experience painful confusion even in the face of their radical commitment.

No, the obvious comparison is too narrow and too easy. The examples of purified identity cited before reveal, in an extreme form, something nascent in more ordinary adolescent life. Adolescence is commonly thought to be a period of wandering and exploration; children become men and women sexually, the shelter of the home for a majority of the young is left behind, the capacity and the desire to act as newly independent beings grows strong. With this enlarging of human horizons in adolescence, it must surely seem inappropriate to see born at the same stage of life those tactics of evasion and avoidance of unknown, painful experiences that give rise to the desire for purity and coherence. Yet certain puzzles in ordinary adolescent behavior can be explained in no other way.

One of these puzzles is the high number of young

people at the point of entering college who fasten on a choice of career without giving themselves a chance to explore alternatives. One study estimates that about three out of every five entering college students choose careers for themselves before having any experience or knowledge of their future pursuits; the striking thing is that relatively few of these students break their initial choice. In talking to students who have so committed themselves, one feels the intense desire many of them have to move out on their own; yet something hidden in themselves, something they can't vocalize, chains them back. In American and English schools, the chains are in part created by their teachers, whose concern for professional work encourages the young to remain in fear of their own power to wander: better solid, if dull, than vital, messy, and a dilettante. But many young people in choosing a life work also chain themselves voluntarily. Many don't want to wander; they want to be sure of what they are doing in advance of doing it.

Another pattern of purification occurs in a curious limitation on adolescent sexuality. From his study of medieval myths of love, Denis de Rougement has suggested that the search for "the" ideal man or woman is a way of avoiding loving real people, since "the" ideal mate is really only a reflection of oneself as one would like to be; it is not another person with a life of his or her own. Yet it is exactly this search for an ideal mate that flowers in adolescent sexuality, that creates its narcissism and homosexual undertow. This search for gods or goddesses to love leads the young so often, as Erik Erikson puts it, to deny the fact of another real person in

14

sexual relations. And since another real person is not consciously present, there need not occur the endless, often painful, rebalancing between two people who are present to love each other; perfect love in adolescence suffers no such intrusions. Anna Freud has observed that the conflicts involved in an intimacy are evaded in adolescence by a rigid selective process; the young take a painful difference to be a proof that a particular partner is not "the" one.

A third pattern of avoidance the young put on their own powers is more a state of mind than a concrete activity like choosing a career or a partner in love. Yet this state of mind is to me the most marked characteristic of adolescent purity concerns. It is the attempt of the young to create an aura of invulnerable, unemotional competence for themselves. Researches into the inner life of juvenile gangs mention this attitude, but its penumbra in adolescence is much wider than the attitudes of tough kids. In the desire to be "on top of things," to control something so totally that nothing occurs outside of one's power, one insulates the experiences one is willing to probe or submit to. In school, for example, it is rare for students to ask each other questions in class, rather than an authority, simply to find something out. Studies of adolescent group life find, instead, a recurrent striving for a "professionalized" expertise in all kinds of activities so that one will not be embarrassed, appear confused, or taken by surprise. But when the dangers of surprise are avoided, there can be no exploration, and so no inner growth.

Indeed, in each of these areas there occurs a voluntary

limitation on the individual's freedom, in order to evade the very fact of growth—the emergence of unknown, and therefore potentially threatening, experiences in a life. It is in such ordinary events as choosing a career or someone to love, or in the common attitude of striving for an invulnerable competence, that the self-imposed limitations of adolescence reveal a desire to purify identity. In these commonplace events is found a desire to establish a coherent and fixed order of life so that the individual may transcend experiences of pain, of dislocation, of being overwhelmed. The question is why growing young people should do this. Why should the fear of experiencing pain result in this particular kind of defense system? The character of these defenses comes, I believe, from a structure peculiar to the adolescent's growth.

Time Scales in Adolescence

It has been said that modern writers on the patterning of human development, like Heinz Hartmann and Erik Erikson, have tried to understand how psychic material is created in the course of a lifetime, rather than revealed, as the older psychoanalytic school would have it. For Erikson, especially, the framing of life stages is not seen as a process where the same psychic material is reworked in different ways over the course of time; Erikson instead envisages a sequence of life crises where new kinds of reality problems, which involve the individual increasingly in wider social spheres as he matures, bring forth separate and distinctive strengths at different points in a life.

The growth that takes form in adolescence is commonly thought of as bodily and sexual; despite the work of Freud, it is often difficult for even educated opinion to accept pubescence as a continuation and elaboration of a sexuality already alive in childhood. The distinctiveness of adolescence occurs on another plane. Writers, including Anna Freud and Peter Blos as well as Erikson and Hartmann, are now trying to understand the kinds of ethical and value-making strengths that seem to grow in distinctive ways during the adolescent phase of life. It is in this area of value-making and value-choosing that the human being during the late phases of adolescence undergoes an important crisis of life.

This crisis entered everyday language as an "identity crisis" (the term was coined by Erikson), and, as is the way of popularized ideas, has lost its specific meaning. Every unhappy child is not having an identity crisis, nor are middle-aged advertising executives who want to be writers. In Erikson's original meaning, the crisis of identity occurs when a young person perceives a conflict between the social materials he can use in his life and his particular ability or desire to use them. A crisis of identity in late adolescence is one of evaluating the relations between the individual's image of himself and his image of the life outside that self. In this way, the crisis of identity is not simply a crisis of "what my personality is like"; it is rather the *conscious* attempt of the growing human being, for the first time, to formulate *rules* or

17

patterns of the relations between a self-image and an image of the world outside the self.

It is this making of rules to define the relations between an individual's sense of himself and his sense of the social world around him that creates the adolescent's newborn feeling of individuality. The young person is now on his own, because he can finally engage in the activity that in his childhood was the font of parental authority: now he can make ethical rules, "appropriate standards of behavior." He has the sexual and intellectual powers to do so; there is only one thing missing, the experience in using these powers. Intolerant of the old parental restraints, anxious to see and understand for himself, he is like a painter with an enormous supply of paints and brushes but no canvas to work on. He has no idea of the use to which he can put the strengths, the materials for life, that he possesses.

Thus situations in which a young person must make a judgment relating his sense of himself and his sense of what lies outside him are fraught with enormous anxiety. This anxiety occurs, for example, in choosing to prepare for a career. Someone entering college is "ready" intellectually and physically, but not at all "ready" in terms of drawing on the experience of using his powers in a wide variety of situations, to choose what he wants as his peculiar life work. Adolescence is a stage of human growth, in other words, in which the time scales of growth are not in harmony. Sexual, intellectual, and perceptual powers grow at a rate far in advance of the fund of experiences the individual possesses.

Some writers on developmental patterns of children

and adolescents believe that this imbalance in adolescent scales of growing brings to a head an imbalance existent throughout the early years of childhood. They look at each stage of maturation as marked by a disparity between what the child can do emotionally, physically, and intellectually, and what he has done with his abilities. Yet it would be a mistake to treat the imbalance in adolescence as similar in kind, though more intense, to what has come before. The nature of what adolescents can do is essentially different from the nature of what children can do. Sexually, the adolescent finds his power entangled in a web of responsibilities and allegiances not experienced by the child. The context of the family as shelter is in his power to destroy. The imbalance between the possibilities for experience and the lessons of experience is so severe that to the young person it seems unrelatable to what he has known in the past. The experiences open to him to create his regions of freedom and bondage are, in sum, essentially different from the experiences of freedom and bondage open to the child.

This is the paradox of adolescence and its terrible unease. So much is possible, yet nothing is happening; lifelong decisions must be made, yet there is little life as the young individual has suddenly come to conceive of it, life in which he is independent, for him to draw on in making up his mind.

One response of young people to this newness and the sense of dislocation and painful disorder it entails is to try to explain the future totally, completely, all at once, in order to gain control over the outpouring of new life and new possibility. This impulse to explain in advance of experience, to collapse the experienced scale of time, what Anna Freud calls the intellectualization of adolescents, is a defense against pain. It assumes the lessons of experience without undergoing the actual experience itself. This peculiar, conscious response to painful dislocation is what generates in adolescence the tools for purifying identity relations.

The defense against pain by a formal insulation of one's relations to the outside has its roots in the way human beings at a certain stage of development, when they are *unavoidably* overwhelmed, as adolescents are, exercise new powers of imagining the rules by which they are related to the world around them. By imagining the meaning of a class of experiences in advance or apart from living them, a young person is freed from having to go through the experience itself to understand its meaning. He makes up the meaning in isolation. This sorting mechanism becomes a curse in the identity crisis, when the collapsing of experience in a young person's mind becomes so strong that it works and serves as a stable substitute for the testing of new powers in unknown conditions. If projection of the meaning of experience does work as a stable substitute, then the young person has actually acquired a powerful weapon to prevent any exposure of himself; in other words, he has learned how to insulate himself in advance from experiences that might portend dislocation and disorder.

In this way, the adolescent can sustain a purified picture of his own identity: it *is* coherent, it is orderly, it is consistent, because he has learned how to exclude disorder and painful disruption from conscious consideration. In this way, forging a coherent identity, by destroying the intrusion of historical experience, by refusing to let it be anything other than what one wants it to be, dissipates the tension in the unequal time scales of growth during adolescence. The result is a language of experience whose terms appear most strikingly in a social process seldom thought of in relation to adolescence.

We are beginning to see in certain social upheavals a familar and depressing character type, a new leader consumed by the desire for a more humane order yet who also reveals a terrible kind of inhumanity, a rigid, insatiable search for a life he can never achieve. The flowering of a pain-transcending, timeless ideal seems to push such leaders to act in ways that contradict the humanity and openness of the specific reforms they espouse.

In the retribution imposed by these revolutionary leaders after their ascension to power, the old leaders can be converted into symbols of a whole host of overwhelming forces the new leaders have felt threatened by. In the Reign of Terror in France, the Girondists were transformed by the Jacobins into symbols of the old regime, although they were fellow, though more moderate, revolutionaries. In Stalin's purges of the 1930's, the cultural revolutionaries of the 1920's were converted into decadent representatives of the dying capitalist spirit. (There is a terrible irony in the extermination of these truly creative figures by a man whose artistic tastes were closest to those of the nineteenth-century bourgeois French.)

Why does this retribution operate through the symbolization of these revolutionaries' enemies? There lies here, I believe, the key to understanding how the purification drives can deal with the immediate world without becoming a part of it.

Unlike a poetic symbol, these symbols of retribution and revenge deny the "factness" of the person on whom they are fastened. A poetic symbol suggests to us, through the concreteness of a thing or person, a broader penumbra of meaning. The symbols of retribution destroy any concrete sense of the thing or person; the man chosen as the symbol of past wrongs has no life of his own in the hearts of his punishers. Through symbolic rhetoric, a millennial leader can strike back at the fact of injury by dealing with the present world without dealing in it. This is the abstractness one senses in the language of men like Robespierre. To get specific would throw into jeopardy the desires that mold a millennial leader.

In this annihilation of the present through a special kind of metaphor, such leaders teach something about the outcome of more ordinary men's desire for purified experience. In ordinary lives, the desire for purity, emerging in adolescence, can lead to a language that similarly does away with the "factness" of new people or new experiences. This occurs most elementally and innocently in the *patois* of adolescents, now a murky combination of white hipsterese and black soul talk: if forty different things are just "a groove," does any of them have a character of its own? But the same process is at work in deeper metaphors of meaning: the framing of an ideal boy or girl is a way of defending against the uniqueness, which is to say the reality, of each boy or girl an adolescent meets, by measuring the real people against the ideal person the adolescent has already decided to be the best for him.

That writers like Blos and Erikson notice an absorption in the oneness of self by adolescents is, again, if we follow the clues from some revolutionary behavior, not surprising. For by turning one's energies to an ideal of oneness, the enemies of purity, the disjointed, confusing experiences of interaction in the everyday world, can be dismissed as of lesser importance, and the young person can, like Malraux's character Hong, imagine himself strong because he refuses to let himself be challenged.

All too often in the past, psychologists and psychiatrists have treated emotional health as a strength diametrically opposed to emotional "disease"—which was taken to be essentially a form of human weakness. The present generation of practitioners is becoming aware of how much emotional "diseases" can be a product of human strengths, strengths that come to be misused in a life, rather than being absent or weakened.

The adolescent configuration described here is such a strength. The young person gains a tool for making a response to the imbalance of his scales of growth. Rather than passively suffering, he brings into being a means for rationalizing and acting as an independent being in a strange milieu. What I intend to show is *not* that this strength is innately bad or "unhealthy," but rather that it is extremely dangerous if it remains fixed in a person's life, if it meets no challenge and becomes a permanent modality. If there is no movement beyond this initial pattern of identity forging, a terrible paradox is created.

Men can abandon any attempts at personal experiment out of the conviction that they already know what any experiment with their own lives will lead to. For making things coherent means imagining they are known and understood by the simple act of an individual's will. Thus the principle of security and regularity comes to be enshrined, through the willful illusion that the young person, or the older person who carries the scar from his youth, has somehow already tested all possibilities open to him. In this way, the forces behind purification, forces of fear, lead the young person to enter adult life in a state of bondage to security, in a self-imposed illusion of knowledge about the outcome of experiences he has never had.

The Desire for Purity, Seen as an Illness

Psychologists tend to view the forces creating this desire for purity, when it becomes totally fixed and dominant in a life, as a form of emotional illness. These forces can affect the way in which people punish themselves for things they feel guilty about. In trying to get a hold on a painful experience for which a man feels guilt, without having to accept it as real, without having to feel its sting, it is common for people to try to disembody the situation through a general metaphor of personal failure or sinfulness. For it is much easier to say that I am a sinner, to make it a transcendent proposition, than to say I hurt this man at this time and place. Thus out of the dynamics of self-purification may come an overwhelming, yet at bottom comforting, sense of guilt that destroys a man's capacity to deal with concreteness in the world. This is a pathological condition, in that it justifies a man in remaining passive in the face of everyday situations and problems, passive as well toward the effects of his actions on other people. Whatever evil he causes he can comfortably tolerate because he postulates himself as a terrible sinner.

But what has not been explored before about the desires for purified experience in adolescence is how they come to be expressed as a community phenomenon. That the adolescent process of making an identity of coherence has a social character can be seen in such areas as adolescent career choice, sexual identity, and the pretensions of emotionless competence. But a communal structure that is built out of desires for purity in adolescence means something more: when the purification desires of a large number of people succeed and become dominant in their lives, it would be only natural for these men to try to mold society in their own image, so that the structure of society would be organized to encourage and to codify this peculiar escape from painful disorder.

To assume the meanings of experience without the threat of actively experiencing—there is nothing so unique about this development in adolescence that its fruits are to be seen only in people who are deviants. Rather, as I shall now try to show, this twisted strength in the cycle of human growth has found its strongest expression today in the ways affluent communities organize repression. For it is the social structure of modern urban communities of affluence that not only prolongs this adolescent pattern of avoidance, but also subsequently works to freeze adult lives in the same pattern, so that men are continually led to imagine meanings about all manner of experience they are afraid to have. The "pathology" here is that, by codifying the desire for coherence in affluent communal life, men have found the means to impose a voluntary slavery upon themselves. It is this slavery their more sensitive children now are fleeing, it is this narrowness by choice that is prompting the young to search for a new kind of community life.

CHAPTER TWO

The Myth of a Purified Community

THE "PROTESTANT ETHIC" WAS A PHRASE MADE FAMOUS in Max Weber's *The Protestant Ethic and the Spirit of Capitalism.* Weber's book has been attacked over and over during the last fifty years, in part because people thought Weber meant by this Protestant ethic a religious philosophy that somehow caused or helped bring into being the spirit of capitalism. Weber meant in fact something simpler and subtler.

Weber saw in the motives for religious belief among certain seventeenth-century Protestant leaders a desire to find in the worldly, everyday acts of men the signs of religious virtue, even as these Protestants believed men in their daily lives were totally ignorant of the divine or the state of their own souls. This contradiction was no abstraction, Weber discovered, for the people living at that time. On the one hand, unlike their Catholic brethren, these men had wiped away the rites by which the divine spoke to them and forgave their sins. The Puritan God was inscrutable. On the other hand, and again unlike the Catholics, they wanted to see in their daily lives some unshakable proofs of their own virtue, so that they would be assured about what awaited them after death. This contradiction made worldly acts terribly important as signs of virtue, and therefore the subject of constant scrutiny and analysis; however, they were also empty, since man could have no knowledge of how God wanted them to act.

Max Weber's great insight was seeing in this religious situation the expression of a kind of anxiety that would lead men to self-denial and self-repression, out of fear of transgressing some sacred code whose rules could not be understood. And Weber perceived that later in history the kinds of men who became capitalists evinced the same kind of anxiety, expressed in remarkably similar form to the Protestants, and especially to those Protestants who were Puritans. Weber deduced that the capitalists, who were a new phenomenon in the eighteenth and nineteenth centuries, might therefore have suffered from the same contradictory problem as earlier faced the Puritans. They were engaged in a meaningless world whose pursuits— i.e., making money—had no value of their own, and yet these pursuits had a great value, in that they were a demonstration of the virtue of those who engaged in them. The Puritan dilemma was repeated as men scrutinized each others' acts for traces of a goodness whose nature the worldly acts could not reveal.

It is this asceticism, this "worldly watching" of the acts of others and oneself for signs of an unknowable virtue, that was the communal expression of the drive for purity among both Puritans and entrepreneurs.

This self-repressive ethic in both cases created community life. In Puritan times people watched each other for signs of doctrinal virtue and vice, in the later era people watched each other and themselves for signs of those qualities of thrift and self-denial that would lead to wealth, wealth that was in turn a sign of virtue no one could quite name.

The reason for the similarity between this particular religious movement and the economic movement that followed was what Weber sought. Both were built out of anxiety, and both led to self-denial and communal repression of unvirtuous activity. Weber's direction was quite clear: he tried to show how a certain kind of drive for purity of self could survive, as a social value, in an age that had put aside religion.

But at this point Weber left the phenomenon. The image of a puritanical ethic, a worldly asceticism as he called it, was drawn no further in his account than the communal life of the eighteenth century. Yet the ingredients that created this ethic—fear, a contradictory system of values, a self-repression designed to be a sign of some personal response to a situation innately out of control—these problems are too deep-seated in men's natures simply to have died out.

A New Puritan Ethic

The last chapter showed how in adolescence there arise
contradictions in growth leading to a peculiar kind of fear.
This fear in turn leads to a pattern of self-denial and an
avoidance of risk in identity patterns. The impact of this
process is the possibility for ordinary adolescents and the
probability for some adolescents and adults that they
would establish permanent tools for purifying their experience of the fearful or unknown. It would be natural
to ask what relation this psychological process in adolescence has to the cultural "ethic" of self-denial that
Weber found in the Puritans and early capitalists of the
past. The answer, I believe, is that this adolescent process
has created, in modern times, a community ethic of purity
dramatically different from the communities produced
by worldly asceticism in the past.

I hesitate to say that different historical uses have been
made of the same adolescent crisis, for the psychology of
individuals is itself historical, not immutably given. Instead, I think the psychological ideas about self-denial
developed since Weber's time provide the tools for understanding a new kind of "puritan ethic" in community life.
To understand what this new puritan ethic is, this new
desire for purity in communal affairs, something needs to
be said about the idea of community itself.

"Community" is a deceptive social term. People speak
of a "community" of interest—for instance, men who do
the same kind of labor or depend on each other to make

money. There are also "communities" of affection, like churches or ethnic groups whose members feel emotional ties to one another. Yet, even in everyday language, the idea of a community is not interchangeable with the idea of a social group; a community is a particular kind of social group in which men believe they *share* something together. The feeling of community is fraternal, it involves something more than the recognition that men need each other materially. The bond of community is one of sensing common identity, a pleasure in recognizing "us" and "who we are."

The emotions involved in this feeling of solidarity are complex, and writers on society understand little about them. At the opening of this century, the German social thinker Ferdinand Tönnies tried to sketch out the differences between a community life, in which people felt emotional ties with each other as full human beings, and group life, in which men felt their ties in terms of emotionally neutral, specialized tasks they performed together. The generation Tönnies taught tended to view this split between community and group as opposite poles of social experience. In the great flowering of sociology at the University of Chicago in the decades following the First World War, writers such as Robert Park, Louis Wirth, and Robert Redfield began to cast the differences between the two as the differences between village and city. While in village life men felt they belonged together and shared with each other in the full range of human activity, in the city, said these writers, men came to feel a part of each other's lives by virtue of functional tasks performed in common; the tasks were themselves so specialized that men's feeling of relatedness was split into innumerable fragments. In the city, complex emotional interactions between men would only get in the way of doing the specialized tasks.

The trouble with this idea of two poles—village-community versus city-group—is that it has proved itself too neat, too logical, and too simple to account for the varieties of community solidarity. For what modern researchers have uncovered, particularly in affluent city and suburban areas, is that men frame for themselves a belief in emotional cohesion and shared values with each other that has little to do with their actual social experiences together. The specific contents of this belief is the new puritan ethic.

In the years following the Second World War, social researchers such as David Riesman and Maurice Stein became convinced that the feeling of common identity in community life, the projection of threads uniting a group of people, could occur *in advance* of any communal experience between the people involved. This striking idea Riesman carried a step farther when he suggested that the need to project a common character of community life often comes to be at war with the actual way men act with each other. He saw people projecting an image of "who we are," as a collective personality, on a wholly different plane from, and in advance of, the character of what they shared.

One striking portrayal of such a community was made a decade ago by Arthur Vidich and Joseph Bensman, who went to live in and study a small town in New York State. They found the people of this community had lives split between pursuits in town and pursuits in a nearby large city; they found that community participation and decision making in the town was shared by only a small number of people; they found such social forces as class, ethnic background, and age to play decisive roles in cutting off contacts between people in the community. And yet, the people of this small town voiced a strong, almost desperate, belief in themselves as a unified group with warm and sustained contacts between all the members of the town community. The actual contacts were mainly centered on discussing the status and the varying fortunes of town members; but these people believed themselves engaged with each other in a much wider, more important way, and they reacted with hostility when challenged by the researchers on the degree of their cohesion. This feeling of solidarity the Polish sociologist Florian Znaniecki calls a community cemented by an act of will rather than by acts of experience.

This same projection of community solidarity, opposed to community experience, struck me forcibly in looking into the chain of events leading to the ouster of a prosperous black family from a wealthy suburb outside a midwestern city. In this suburb the rate of divorce was about four times the national average, the rate of juvenile crime began to approach the worst sections of the city to which it was attached, the incidence of hospitalization from emotional collapse was frequent. Yet the people of the community united in a great show of force to drive the black family from its home three days after it had moved in because the residents said, among other things, that "we are a community of solid families" and "we don't want the

kind of people in who can't keep their families together."
"This is a happy, relaxed place," one resident said, "and
the character of the community has to be kept together."
The importance of this incident isn't simply *that* the residents of the suburb lied, but why they lied in this particular way.

Some writers have argued that "insecurity" as such is
at the root of this need for an image of community, of
"us." Talcott Parsons, for instance, has made a brilliant
study along these lines in discussing the need of the Nazi
Germans to define something characteristically "Aryan."
During periods of social change and displacement, these
writers say, the desire grows strong to define a common
"us" so that men may forge a bulwark for themselves
against disorder.

But putting the matter in this way brings up something
we have already discussed in terms of individual growth:
the purifying of identity may be forged in a life as a
means of evading experiences that can be threatening,
dislocating, or painful. Is there a connection between this
community by an act of will, this identity of a coherent
"us," and the tools generated in adolescents by which individuals acquire a purified "me," resistant to new experience?

The connection exists, I believe, and is unlike what
Weber observed in the communities of the Puritan world.
For here the images of communal solidarity are forged in
order that men can avoid dealing with each other, while
in the Puritan sects or among the early entrepreneurs the
images of purity were constructed so that men might
come closer to one another and justify new kinds of social

34

actions. The asceticism Weber saw in germ in the Puritan world, with its constant mutual interrogation and examination, and the worldly asceticism of the next century, where men scrutinized each other's activity to find the signs of grace in those virtues leading to wealth—these attempts to purify the self led men into a community of experience, to use Znaniecki's phrase. But the mechanisms of repression Vidich and Bensman found were myths that kept men from having to interact and understand each other as they really were. The Puritan's community life or that of the struggling entrepreneurs did not exclude conflict; in fact, conflict was often encouraged for attaining virtuous ends. The small town in upstate New York and the suburb where "bad" black families were excluded feared conflict because conflict involved confrontation between men, friends as well as enemies, and that was an uncontrollable and therefore threatening social event. By an act of will, a lie if you like, the myth of community solidarity gave these modern people the chance to be cowards and hide from one another.

There is also a great economic difference in the fantasies of community identity Riesman, Vidich, and Stein found. These fantasies have taken place in relatively affluent communities. Affluence, as shall be seen, gives a community new tools to define itself in this particular way. It is also affluence that makes this problem in community life one to be faced by post-revolutionary societies that manage to survive as well as by the societies of the West. For especially in affluent communities the particular feeling of nonexperienced solidarity is a logical use of the powers developed in adolescence to avoid pain.

How the Myth of Community Purity Is Formed

The feeling of a common identity, in the forms Riesman and Znaniecki describe, is a counterfeit of experience. People talk about their understanding of each other and of the common ties that bind them, but the images are not true to their actual relations. But the lie they have formed as their common image is a usable falsehood—a myth—for the group. Its use is that it makes a coherent image of the community as a whole: people draw a picture of who they are that binds them all together as one being, with a definite set of desires, dislikes, and goals. The image of the community is purified of all that might convey a feeling of difference, let alone conflict, in who "we" are. In this way the myth of community solidarity is a purification ritual.

Involved here is a collapsing of the experiential frame, a condensing of all the messy experiences in social life, in order to create a vision of unified community identity. It is exactly this detour around social contact and experience in the making of a coherent common identity that reveals the marks of adolescence on the community process.

Adolescence has been described as a stage of life in which the individual finally attains his full range of human powers, but is empty of adult-like experience to guide him in using those powers. This imbalance in the time scales of growth is particularly acute in the realm of ethical and social choices. Young people have the power to be free, to choose their future careers, to explore themselves outside the boundaries of family and school, to have full and diverse erotic relations; but they sense no history of freedom under these terms in their own lives. This is the hidden malaise, as I understand it, behind what writers like Erikson call a crisis of identity. Some adolescents do have the strength to hold themselves back, and let a diversity of painful, confused, and contradictory new experiences enter their lives, before they take the active steps that will confirm them in an identity. But most young people are denied the strength to endure ambiguity of this kind, and exercise their new powers to form *conscious* meanings and value relations to themselves about experiences they are yet to have. In this way, the experiential frame is controlled in advance; its impact on the reality a youth perceives is muffled because unexpected or painful new experiences are rejected as unreal. They don't fit into the schemes of coherent order the young person is now able to articulate consciously to himself.

It is the same projection—a picture of "us" as a coherent being in advance of actual social relations—that links the feeling of communal solidarity to the patterns of avoidance learned in adolescence. Certain tools of avoidance used by a human being to deal with crises in his own growth patterns are subsequently transferred to the way he understands himself as a social being. This transfer of a skill learned in adolescence is how the myth of a purified community comes into being.

The illusion retained by adolescents caught by the desire for purified identity is that they chose a coherent

37

and secure routine with knowledge and experience of all the alternatives to security. There is no reason why people, having learned such a technique of avoidance in their individual lives, could not learn as adults to share it together. Communally painful experiences, unknown social situations full of possible surprise and challenge can be avoided by the common consent of a community to believe they already know the meaning of these experiences and have drawn the lessons from them together. For example, in the suburb that expelled its wealthy black family, the myth the white residents created—that they were voluntarily a tight-knit group of stable families—served to make them immune in advance to the pain of dealing concretely and directly with the black family. Because the whites felt as one in their illusion about their family stability, they could drive out people they presumed to be different.

It is a truism among students of small groups that people feel most uneasy and most challenged by perceiving the "otherness" of the people around them. Finding the differences between oneself and the world outside oneself seems to be much more difficult to bear than finding the points of similarity. The fear of "otherness," of that which one does not know, is exactly of a piece with what men fear about *themselves* and their own powers when those powers ripen in adolescence. From adolescence people take a power for mythmaking into their adult community lives to blunt the conscious perception of "otherness."

A community is not simply a social group or an unrelated collection of individuals living in the same place. It is a group in which people belong to each other, share

something in common. What is distinctive about this
mythic sharing in communities is that people feel they
belong to each other, and share together, because they are
the same. The narrowness of this feeling can best be seen
by contrasting it to the sharing and sense of belonging
in a strong love. As Denis de Rougemont has so wisely
remarked, the sharing that occurs in deep relations of
intimacy grows out of loving the distinctiveness, the
uniqueness of the other person, not in the merging of
selves into one homogenized being. But in the purification
of a coherent community image, fear rather than love of
men's "otherness" prevails. Out of this fear is bred the
counterfeit of experience. The "we" feeling, which expresses a desire to be similar, is a way for men to avoid
the necessity of looking deeper into each other; instead,
men imagine that they know all about each other, and
their knowledge becomes a vision of how they must be the
same.

In this way the "we" feeling can grow up among people
whose lives strike the outsider as so disparate in actuality,
who seem in fact to share very little with each other and
matter very little in each other's lives. It is this counterfeit sense of community that Stein, Riesman, Vidich, and
Znaniecki have described. The counterfeit is not bred, I
believe, out of peculiarities in local or even American conditions. Rather it is bred out of the way human beings
learn at a certain point in their own growth how to lie to
themselves, in order to avoid new experiences that might
force them to endure the pain of perceiving the unexpected, the new, the "otherness" around them. Through
this peculiar learning process "belonging" to one another

becomes a shared sense of what we think we ought to be like, as one social being, in order not to be hurt.

But resolving the fear of "otherness" through this myth of solidarity affects the ways the community, as an entity in itself, will operate over the course of time.

The Social Structure of the Myth

The myth of solidarity in community life speaks to a more complex human problem than social conformity. Usually discussions of conformity to mass values and mores have treated the human beings involved as being, at their very worst, passive creatures manipulated by an impersonal system. Thus is there supposed conformity without pleasure, mindless obedience to the norms. This is much too flattering a picture of the human impulses at work.

When the desire for communal sameness is understood as the exercise of powers developed in everyday life rather than as the fruit of some abstract creature called "the system" or "mass culture," it is inescapable that the people involved in this desire for coherence *actively* seek their own slavery and self-repression. They would be insulted if the issue were stated so boldly, of course; yet it is their acts, their impulses that create the communal forms. The social images do not materialize out of thin air; they are made by men, because men have learned in their individual lives, at one stage of development, the very tools of avoiding pain later to be shared together in a repressive, coherent, community myth.

When the French writer Alexis de Tocqueville came to America a century and a half ago, he was struck by the grip this repressive myth had on American community life. The Americans he observed needed to be assured by each other that they were the same—that is, *equal in condition*. Tocqueville believed they felt this need because they felt insecure about their own dignity as men; the act of drawing together, in confirming to each other their sameness and their coherence in a common image, warded off the apprehension of threatened dignity. The issues so far explored could be expressed in Tocqueville's terms, as a way men counterfeit a feeling of dignity through an image of equality. There is born in adolescence, and subsequently reified in community life, a means of reassuring oneself that the process of learning about life has occurred even as the substance of learning is avoided. The result is a feeling of dignity in the image of sameness, of equality of condition, as Tocqueville put it, that men forge for themselves.

There are three marked social consequences of this myth of dignity through communal solidarity.

The first is the loss of actual participation in community life, the loss of situations of confrontation and exploration between individual groups of men. Tocqueville believed this occurred because the individuals of the community convinced themselves that since the community was in hands much like their own, no matter who ruled, the community was in good hands. If each man was dignified, and if all shared the same character, then all were dignified and could be trusted. Thus men could return to their real concerns, Tocqueville said, which were the petty, routine, isolated pleasures of everyday life. Solidarity in name and isolation in fact were, Tocqueville said, cause and effect.

But I believe the psychological ideas of this essay put the matter in a different way. Innate to the process of forming a coherent image of community is the desire to avoid actual participation. Feeling common bonds without common experience occurs in the first place because men are afraid of participation, afraid of the dangers and the challenges of it, afraid of its pain. Therefore, withdrawing from participation is not simply a possibility under these conditions, as Tocqueville believed; it is the driving power that produces the urge of men to feel socially alike, to share a myth of common identity.

Thus, in the wealthy suburb whose residents were suddenly faced with the possibility of having to deal with a real situation—the introduction of a prosperous black family in their midst—the racial prejudice was a product of something in the lives of the suburbanites themselves, something that had little to do with their feelings about blacks. The racial prejudice was a cover for their fear of having to be social beings, to deal with each other in order to cope. In order to defend against this social participation, and all its pain, they had to proclaim a lie about who they were, about their own coherent and unified community image. This resulted in a lie about the corresponding "otherness" of blacks.

The incident suggests a second consequence of the feeling of coherence in a community: the repression of deviants. Again, Tocqueville saw the brute repression of deviants as a necessity if men were to keep convincing themselves of their collective dignity through their collective sameness. The "poets of society," the men who challenged the norms, would have to be silenced so that sameness could be maintained. But when the "we" feeling is understood as a myth bred in the life cycle, the repression a community practices is more than just a means to an end; in fact, it is exactly the same process of repression that the majority, the "we," exercise against themselves. We do not expel this black family from our neighborhood in order to make the neighborhood a nicer place, although that is what we tell ourselves. In the end, the blacks could be blue or brown or green; what we are afraid of is that something "other" will come to matter to us, and then we might be hurt by our own exploration of "otherness."

So the expressions of common identity and the repression of deviants are both aspects of men's fear of power within themselves. To permit the freedom of deviation would be to care about the unknown, the other, in social contacts. The myths of community are self-destructive in that they take a strength developed on the eve of adulthood and use it to repress other human strengths, like curiosity and the desire to explore.

The term "repression" is today becoming a generalized catchword in intellectual circles the way "communist" was once among anti-intellectuals. As Kai Erikson has pointed out, total repression of deviants would rob society of a means of defining itself; there must be room for "them" for "us" to exist as well. But the myth of a common "us" *is* an act of repression, not simply because it excludes outsiders or deviants from a particular community, but because of what it requires of those who are the elect, the included ones. The elect must give up complex or conflicting loyalties, and they *want* to do this, want to become slaves to each other, in order to avoid the strengths in themselves that would make them explorers beyond comfortable limits.

The third consequence of this desire for an image of coherent, shared community life lies in its relation to violence.

The myth of community solidarity disposes men, I believe, to escalate discord with other communities or with outsiders too powerful to be excluded to the level of violent confrontation. Essentially, communities whose people feel related to each other by virtue of their sameness are polarized. When issues within or without the community arise that cannot be settled by routine processes of bureaucratic administration, it seems that the whole fabric of the myth is in jeopardy because of an intractable issue or event that cannot be assimilated. This occurs because the basis of community order is community sameness; problems that can't fit the mold challenge the feeling of being together because of being alike. In situations like these, everyone's dignity is threatened, and people can't ignore it. They feel that the very survival of the community is at stake, and in a sense they are right. Individuals in the community have achieved a coherent sense of themselves precisely by avoiding painful experiences, disordered confrontations and experiments, in their own identity formation. Having, therefore, so little tolerance for disorder in their own lives, and having shut themselves off so that they have little experience of disorder as well, the eruption of social tension becomes a situation in which the ultimate methods of aggression, violent force and reprisal, seem to become not only justified, but life-preserving. It is a terrible paradox that the escalation of discord into violence comes to be, in these communities, the means by which "law and order" should be maintained.

In this way some communities, through such tools as the police, respond totally out of proportion to the provocations they receive. I am not thinking here so much of the obvious examples—Chicago during the Democratic National Convention, the Mexican student uprising of 1968, the recent purges in Chinese cities—as of subtle processes, like the reactions in most American suburbs after the chain of riots from 1964 to 1968. These riots, unlike most insurrectionary outbreaks, did not burst the boundaries of the black ghettos; they never involved mass shootings or mobs storming government centers; rather they focused on the seizure of small articles of property, food, or liquor. As one North Vietnamese revolutionary is said to have remarked, they were not so much a revolt as an apocalyptic, despairing act of self-destruction by people who felt they could bear no more. However, the reaction in the white suburbs was that "we" were threatened, that blacks were spilling out of the ghettos, that actual civil war and personal attack were imminent. Gun sales in the suburbs rose sharply, grandmothers began to learn how to shoot to kill, liberals suddenly began to understand the "logic" of the separatist movement, the police were unleashed in the cities in a wave of violent reprisals and mindless destructiveness. The overwhelming feeling of "us" being mortally threatened, so incommensurate, so out of touch with the actual tragedy of self-destruction, is the puzzle of these civil disorders. This kind of reaction, this inability to deal with disorder without raising it to the scale of mortal combat, is inevitable when men shape their common lives so that their only sense of relatedness is the sense in which they feel themselves to be the same. It is because men are uneasy and intolerant with ambiguity and discord in their own lives that they do not know how to deal with painful disorder in a social setting, and instead escalate disorder to the level of life or death struggle.

And finally, the economic environment of abundance in a community strengthens each of these consequences of the urge toward community coherence.

The Role of Abundance in the Myth

One recurrent image in the language of society is the great, teeming chaos of cities. Its fascination and its terror come from the diversity within the city's borders; the garment district of New York, for example, spills into a district of offices which spills into a district of social-work agencies which spills into a district of elegant townhouses which spills finally into the great shopping areas around Fourteenth Street. Anyone walking through this diversity in lower midtown feels an enormous vibrancy in the over-lap of so many different kinds of life. This diversity was created in the history of New York because none of these areas of activity had enough power to control its own limits as a community. None of them was rich and cen-tralized enough to wall itself off, and so each suffered the intrusion of others by necessity.

As Jane Jacobs has observed, this penetration of diverse modes of labor and life into each other has been a char-acteristic feature of the neighborhoods of great American cities, but a characteristic that is in the process of dying off. The reason it is dying lies, I believe, in the role abun-dance plays in forming communities of self-conscious solidarity.

Material abundance in a community provides the power for enforcing a myth of coherent community life. It does so in two ways. The first, and obvious one, is that a com-munity with adequate monetary resources can materially control its boundaries and internal composition. The old neighborhoods in cities were complex precisely because no one group had the economic resources to shield itself; the brownstone dwellers did not have the money to live one family to a house, and so shield the housing unit from influences outside the circle of one family; residential life in turn could not be shielded from commerce, much as people might have wanted to get away from the noisy bars and shops on the first floors of city buildings. People simply hadn't the resources to move out. An economy of scarcity in cities has, at least historically, defied myths of coherence in community affairs; people haven't had the cash to realize their own desires.

Now, with the advent of large sectors of the urban population achieving modest wealth for themselves, those desires for coherence, for structured exclusion and internal sameness, can be played out. Whole urban regions can be divided geographically by class, by race, by ethnicity; "unsightly" activities like stores and entertainment can be hidden from home life, so that community identity through a brutal simplifying of human activities is achieved.

But abundance plays a subtler and perhaps more dangerous role in shaping the desire for a common identity. For in communities that are poor, or in times of scarcity, sharing between individuals and families is a *necessary* element of survival. The sharing of scarce appliances, like a vacuum cleaner, or even of such basic necessities as food, has often been remarked on by visitors to the black ghettos of American cities; historically, however, the same communal sharing, which brings people together and necessitates direct social contacts between them, has been a feature of many diverse city neighborhoods; services, skills, and possessions that could be shared provided a focus for concrete communal activities.

It is the hallmark of abundance that the need for such sharing disappears. Each family has its own vacuum cleaner, its own set of pots and pans, its own transport, supply of water, heat, etc. Thus the necessity for social interaction, the necessity to share, is no longer a driving force in communities of abundance; men can withdraw into their self-contained, self-sustaining homes. This means that the feeling of community, of being related and bound together in some way, is cut off from a region that in the past furnished communal experiences. When much less *must* be shared, there is a much smaller fund of experiences on which individuals can draw to assay the character of each other. In framing a sense of communal bonds, men are inclined much more easily to envisage how they are the same rather than what they actually do in their relations with each other.

Abundance, in other words, increases the power to create isolation in communal contacts at the same time that it opens up an avenue by which men can easily conceive of their social relatedness in terms of their similarity rather than their need for each other.

These are the dimensions of the myth of communal solidarity. It appears as something possible, even probable, in men's lives, as a result of experiences in adolescence. But the myth is more than just a logical social possibility of psychic growth. It is a real force in modern social life, and it has a special relationship to the development of cities during this century. The gradual dominance of this myth is the hidden story behind the community patterns that have been evolving in cities during the last seventy years.

CHAPTER THREE

───❦───

How Cities Bring the Myth to Life

PEOPLE TALK OF THE "URBAN CRISIS" OR THE "URBAN revolution" as though the city had suddenly loomed up as an important focus of social life; the real revolution in city life, though, is the opposite of this popular conception. We face an urban "crisis," if that hackneyed word must be used, because something is dying out in city life at the present time, not because the cities are growing. And the elements of urban life present seventy or a hundred years ago are dying in such a way that the myths of a purified community have come to shape and stultify the city.

Intellectuals are prone to romanticize the past, so that when one speaks of something dying out historically it means the dead past was better. That is a peculiar blindness of much utopian thinking; since the past was better than the present, the future ought to restore the past. Such is not my intention: what can be learned from the condition of city life fifty or seventy years ago is perspective about what is missing today, not a guide for how good cities in the future can be built. In this way, my own thinking has come to diverge from that of Jane Jacobs, in her strong and incisive book *The Death and Life of Great American Cities*. For she makes of the past an era of small, intimate relations between neighbors in city life, and sees that condition as one to be restored. This revival, as I shall try to show, can never be; we need to find some condition of urban life appropriate for an affluent, technological era.

To say that city life is dying out may seem on the surface an absurd proposition. The population of metropolitan regions has grown at a fast rate, principally in a new kind of urban area, the middle-class suburb. All the technology of the city—building, transport, communications systems—has grown immensely in the last seventy years. We are an age which believes that if technology and administrative complexity are growing, then "society" as such must be becoming more vital. Thus the city appears on the surface to be an ever more complex and important institution.

But when future generations of historians come to write the chronicle of this era, they may well note that its most marked feature was the gradual simplification of social interactions and forums for social exchange, underlying an ever-increasing elaboration of technological and bureaucratic systems. It may appear in the future that men of this era balanced their energies in a peculiar way, so that the enthusiasm with which they invented the tools for conducting life in a complex society was balanced by a sluggish lassitude in applying the tools for truly social purposes.

How such a paradox came about is the subject of this chapter. I should say I began to think about this problem by accident. In my own researches on modern family life in the United States, I began to realize a few years ago that the evolution of affluent suburban families in America permitted certain myths of solidarity to take hold, permanently, in the way both parents and children dealt with each other. I was led to reflect on what confluence of family structure, city development, and the new conditions of affluence tended to create this psychological pattern. My thinking had no clarity until I realized that in the last decades the family has appropriated the social functions and contacts that men once sought in the broader arena of the city. This appropriation by the family of social "spaces" once felt inappropriate for the home has encouraged something perverse in the urban communal relations men have left, and in the family itself. This perversity is a seeking after solidarity and a fear of experiences that might create complexity or disorder. The theme of this chapter is that as the family and family-type relations men visualize for themselves in cities have become important, the purification patterns of adolescence are encouraged to take root in both the community and in the individual lives of family members. The result of this process is a duality: social life becomes more primitive, in the quest for a mythic solidarity, even as the technological resources for more complex social structures increase.

For people who grew up on New York's lower East Side, or in the ethnic slums of Boston, or in the terrible industrial towns of England, this idea may seem to indicate a cruel indifference to what it once meant to be poor. Poverty was not beautiful for them: few slum romantics have lived in slums. But there were hidden threads of social structure in those poor city areas, threads that gave the people who lived there other regions of identity beyond the fact of their own poverty. Essentially, the last few decades of prosperity have righted the economic injustice these city people suffered, but at the cost of the breakup of their group life. It is this group life of the past that gives a fresh perspective on the patterns of social interaction that now pervade the cities.

Multiple Contact Points

Let us take a tour down Halstead Street, the center of Chicago's great immigrant ghetto, around 1910. The street was twenty-two miles long, and for the most of it filled with a teeming population. Were we to start at its northern end and move south, we would be conscious that it was filled with "foreigners," but at every place with different kinds of foreigners, all mixed together. A native might tell us that a certain few blocks were Greek or Polish or Irish, but were one actually to look at particular houses or apartment buildings, one would find the ethnic groups jumbled together. Even on the Chinese blocks of the street—for the Chinese are supposed at this time to have been the most closed of ethnic societies—there would be numerous families from Ireland or eastern Europe.

The functioning of all these groups on Halstead Street would appear hopelessly tangled to modern observers. For the apartments would be mixed in with stores, the streets themselves crowded with vendors and brokers of all kinds; even factories, as we moved to the southern end of Halstead Street, would be intermixed with bars, brothels, synagogues, churches, and apartment buildings. In the midst of this jumble, there were some hidden threads of a structured social existence.

Were we to follow one of the residents of Halstead Street through a typical day, the experience would be something like this: up at six in the morning, a long walk or a streetcar ride to the factory, and then ten or eleven hours of grueling work. With this much of his day we would be familiar. But when the whistle to stop work blew at six in the evening, his life would take on a dimension perhaps not immediately recognizable. For the path from the factory back home might be broken by an hour's relaxation at a tavern or coffee house. Halstead Street was crammed in 1900 with little cafés where men would come after work to let the tension drain out; talking to friends or reading a newspaper. Dinner would usually be at home, but after dinner the man, sometimes with his wife, would be out of the house again, attending a union meeting, caring for a sick member of a mutual-aid society to which he belonged, or just visiting the apartment of friends. Occasionally, when the family needed some special help, there would be a glass of beer shared with the local political boss, and a plea for assistance—a soft job for an infirm relative, help with a naturalization form, some influence in getting a friend out of jail. Religious responsibilities as well pulled the man and woman out of the house—particularly if they were Jewish or practicing Catholics. The synagogues and churches had to be built in this strange city, and the money and organization to build them could come only from the little men who were their members.

The life of a child on Halstead Street in 1910 would also have been different from what we might expect. The child of ten or eleven would be wakened early in the morning, scrubbed, and sent off to school. Until three in the afternoon he would sit at a high desk, reciting and memorizing. This experience is not alien to us, but again, his life after school would be. For if he did not come home to work, and many did not, he would be out on Halstead Street selling or hawking in the stall of someone much older, who sold and cajoled the passing traffic just as he did. It is amazing to see in old photographs of Halstead Street the young and old, shoulder to shoulder in these stalls, shouting out the prices and the virtues of their wares. Many youths would, with the tacit consent of their parents, enter into the more profitable after-school activity of stealing—we read, for instance, in the letters of one Polish family of great religious piety, of the honor accorded to a little son who had stolen a large slab of beef from a butcher on the corner. Life was very hard and everyone had to fight for their needs with whatever weapons were at hand.

What was contained in this life on Halstead Street could be called a multiplicity of "contact points" by which these desperately poor people entered into social relations with the city. They *had* to make this diversity in their lives, for no one of the institutions in which they lived was capable of self-support. The family depended on political "favors," the escape valve of the coffee shops and bars, the inculcation of discipline of the *shuls* and churches, and so forth, for ongoing support. The political machines tended in turn to grow along family lines, to interact with the shifting politics of church and synagogue. This multiplicity of contact points often took the individuals of the city outside the ethnic "subcultures" that supposedly were snugly encasing them. Polish people who belonged to steel unions often came into conflict with Polish people who had joined the police. This multiplicity of contact points meant that loyalties became crossed in complex forms. The idea of an ethnic "ghetto culture" is not meaningful in describing these men, if the term implies a coherent set of activities and clear-cut affiliations.

This condition has been carefully described by the great Chicago urbanist, Louis Wirth, in his essay "Urbanism as a Way of Life." He tried to show in this essay how the city of necessity broke apart the self-contained qualities of the various ethnic groups. The groups were not like little villages massed together in one spot on the map; rather they penetrated into each other, so that the daily life of an individual was a journey between various kinds of group life, each one different in its function and character from the others. The subtlety of this idea can be seen by comparing a city subculture, as Wirth observed it, to the structure of village culture from which the ethnic groups came. As Robert Redfield and, in a different context, Oscar Handlin, have shown, the salient character of small-village life was the accessibility of all its activities to all members of the village community; the culture of the village was pervasive because there were no disconnected or isolated social regions. Although there was division of labor and rank, the character of the separate activities was known to everyone. What made the ethnic subcultures Wirth wrote about seem different was that the separate activities, or different groups, depended on one another but were not necessarily harmoniously related. Each piece of the city mosaic had a distinct character, but the pieces were "open," and this was what made life urban. Individuals had the capacity and the need to penetrate a number of social regions in the course of daily activities, even though the regions were not harmoniously organized and may even have been at warring ends.

It is our stereotyped thinking about "working class" or "ethnic" culture that inhibits us from seeing the kind of variety cities possessed in the past. We make the life into the image of a village when in fact it was more complex, less unitarily organized. No easy myth of solidarity could develop out of this, no simplicity in a concept of who I am by what I do and what I believe.

It is this multiplicity of contact points that has died out in the city; in its stead, social activities have come to be formed in a more coherent mold.

The Narrowing of Contact Points:
Changes in the Family

In the last half century, a majority of the ethnic groups in the city have achieved a state of prosperity for themselves far beyond what the first immigrants ever dreamed of. This upward movement in material wealth has been matched by social withdrawal, wherein the older forms of complex association have been replaced by a simpler kind of contact structure. This new pattern is embodied in the growth of a specially strong and intense family life. To understand why the old pattern of multiple contact points died, one needs to know what kind of power this new family life possesses.

When I first began to do research on the structure of city family life, I encountered over and over a popular stereotype: the idea that city conditions somehow contribute to the instability of the home. Evidently, the assumption is that the diversity of the city threatens the security and attachment family members feel for each other. Especially as suburban community life has come to dominate cities, there has grown up a mythological family image of affluent homes where Dad drinks too much, the kids are unloved and turn to drugs, divorce is rampant, and breakdowns are routine. The good, old, rural families, by contrast, were supposedly loving and secure.

The trouble with this popular image is that it simply isn't true. Talcott Parsons has amassed evidence to show that the rate of divorce and desertion was much higher "in the good old days," at the turn of the century, than it is now. William Goode has taken the idea a step further by showing how divorce is *less* frequent in affluent homes than in working-class homes. There may still be a great deal of unrest and tension in these suburban families, but it cannot be allied to their structural instability. In fact, we shall see, it is the juncture of great formal stability with deep and unresolved tension that now marks these families; and it is these permanent families, with their unspoken and unresolved divisions, that have come to hunger after a mythic ideal of social solidarity.

The idea of the city weakening the family has also come to express itself in the popular perversions of the Moynihan Report on the family lives of the black ghettos. This document is actually about the impact of unemployment on family structure. It has been misread, however, as a description of how Northern city life has broken apart the black family, and is taken in a most perverted form as a sign that there is something too "weak" in black culture to enable it to withstand the terrors of the city. Actually the phenomenon Moynihan describes occurs wherever unemployment or intermittent employment is a long-term family experience. One therefore finds a much higher rate of female-headed households, with shifting male partners and "illegitimate" children, among persecuted rural Catholics in Northern Ireland than among the blacks of New York City. But the myth remains: somehow it is the big city that has done this.

This stereotype—the threat to family solidarity posed by the city—I investigated in my book *Families Against the City* for a group of middle-class people in Chicago at the end of the nineteenth century. What happened to these people was exactly opposite to the stereotype of family-city relations. For the disorder and vigor of Chicago life at that time pushed these families in upon themselves, as a means of defense against the diversity of the city. They became, in the words of Theodore Dreiser, "little islands of propriety," self-contained, intense, and narrow in their outlook, self-restrictive and routine in the tenor of their family activities. They became safe places in the city at the cost of becoming suffocatingly dull.

The striking historical character of these families was not their intensity as such, but their isolation. That is, what makes them different from the middle-class families of our time, and different from the poor immigrants of their own day, was that they were almost totally islands, and had little contact with other families or small groups in their neighborhood. That kind of family isolation has abated; in times of crisis, families now in a neighborhood develop temporary bonds for mutual aid. But an increasing body of data is showing that the intensity, the inward-turning qualities of day-to-day family life have not died out but have continued over the course of time. In fact, the direction of historical change in the city has been for large numbers of families, including the newly affluent working-class sector and the upwardly mobile segments of the black community, to come to share this characteristic once typical of the native-born, urban middle class.

What is meant by an "intense" family life? The condition of middle-class family intensity that has passed down over the last century is defined by two structural characteristics. The first is that the interactions which occur in the family are taken as a microcosm of all the kinds of interaction that exist in the social world at large. There is nothing really "important" in social relations that cannot be experienced within the boundaries of the home. Men who believe this conceive, therefore, of no reason for making social forays or social contacts that cannot be ultimately reconciled or absorbed in family life.

The second structure creating intense family life is the reduction of family members to levels of equality. This characteristic is much more pronounced in American urban families than European ones. The feeling consists, most vulgarly, in fathers wanting to be "pals" to their sons, and mothers sisters to their daughters; there is a feeling of failure and dishonor if the parents are excluded from the circle of youth, as though they were tarnished by being adult. A good family along these lines is a family where the people talk to each other as equals, where the children presume to the lessons of experience, and the parents try to forget them. That the dignity of all the family members might lie exactly in mutual respect for separateness and uniqueness is not conceived; dignity is conceived to lie in treating everyone equally. This brings the family members into a closer relation to each other—for there are taken to be, ideally, no unbridgeable gaps.

Both of these structures of intensity have become in fact structures for limiting the diversity of family experience.

The conviction of a family that it is the whole social arena in microcosm limits the experience of family members in both an obvious and a subtle way. It is clear that no congeries of four or five people represents the full spectrum of attitudes and human traits to be found in the wider society. Family reality, therefore, becomes highly exclusive. Studies of intense family attitudes toward strangers reveal that the outsiders are judged to be "real," to be important and dealt with only to the extent that they resemble the limited social configurations within the family circle. The most striking form of this can be seen in situations where middle-class neighborhoods have been successfully integrated racially. The black families have been accepted to the extent that people feel they are after all "just like us," or as a respondent in one study put it: "You wouldn't even know from the way the . . . family acts they were Negroes." Accepting someone *ineradicably* different is not what occurs under these conditions.

The subtle way in which families, feeling themselves a microcosm of the society, become self-limiting has to do with the base of stability on which such families rest. This base is the existence, or the belief in the existence of, long-term trust. For families to believe they are all-important there has to be the conviction that no betrayal and breakup will occur over the long term. People do not concentrate their energies in one place and simultaneously believe it may shatter or betray them. Yet long-term situations of trust and reliability are rare in the larger social world. Not only in work but also in a variety of human affairs there are experiences of power and significance that cannot depend on a mutual commitment or trust for a long period. The older forms of social contact were not predicated along these lines. Now, people refuse to grant worth to that which is shifting, insecure, or treacherous, and yet this is exactly what the diversity in society is built of.

The collapsing of family members to a state of equality often leads, in the same way, to a tragic self-limiting of the experience of family members. A recent project made psychiatric interviews in homes of "normal," "just average" families in a modest suburb outside a large city. Over and again in these interviews adults expressed a sense of loss, sometimes amounting to a feeling of self-destruction, in the things in their lives they had wanted to do and could afford to do, but refrained from experiencing for fear of leaving out the children. These sacrifices were not dictated by money; they were much more intimate, small-scale, yet important things: establishing a quiet spot in the day after work when a man and a woman could be alone together, taking trips or vacations alone, eating dinner after the children were put to bed. In another frame, fathers spoke over and over of how they had failed their sons by not being able to understand them; when the interviewers asked what they meant, the response usually came as a version of "he doesn't open up to me the way he does to his friends." Such burdens are acquired, so many daily chances for a diversity and change of routine are denied, out of the belief in the rightness of treating children as much as equals as possible, especially in early and middle adolescence.

In one way, the belief in the family as a microcosm of the world leads to this will to believe the family members all alike, all "pals." For if the family is a whole world, then somehow the conditions of friendship and comradeship must be established within its borders, and this can only be done by treating all the family members as comrades who can understand each other on the same grounds.

The idea just advanced may seem untrue to the experience many people have had in their own lives, an experience of family tension and estrangement unlike what previous generations of the family seemed to know. But there is a perverse, hidden strain to this family intensity that may make sense of the phenomenon. Perhaps I can illustrate this from some professional work now being done by family researchers.

The Urge for a Purified Identity Hidden in Family Intensity

A few sociologists of the family have recently been at pains to unravel a "guilt over conflict" syndrome. This syndrome appears in the attitudes of many intense-family members toward their families. The syndrome is quite simple to state, and it is quite painful to the people caught in it: good families, upright families, are happy; happiness is usually associated with tranquillity; therefore, when conflicts or fights arise in a family, the family (and the fighter) must be no good, tarnished, and somehow a failure. What sociologists like myself have tried to change is the acceptance by therapists of this syndrome as the correct way to view conflict; the facts indicate that families in which conflicts are held down or suppressed turn out to have much higher rates of deep emotional disorders than families in which conflicts and hostilities are directly and openly expressed.

But the "guilt over conflict" syndrome is significant because it is so deeply held a presupposition about family life: people look at conflicts between generations as an evil, revealing some sort of rottenness in the social fabric, rather than as an inevitable and natural process of historical change. Sharp personality differences within the children's generation, leading to fights or estrangements between brothers and sisters, are viewed as a sign of bad parental upbringing, and so on. Put another way, this anxiety and guilt over family conflict really expresses the wish that diversity and ineradicable differences should not exist in the home, for the sake of social order. And in point of fact one of the most widespread middle-class family diseases is the attempt, usually fatal to a family's "happiness," to suppress divergence and separateness in the growth of family members for the sake of order in the family. It is the intensity of family relations, I believe, that brings this thirst for family order about. For if the family is going to survive as a whole society of its own, the following structures are necessary: an unusual closeness of everyday contact, an attempt to repress the experiential and age differences that naturally would set the family members apart, an attempt to set up assurances of long-term trust and the conviction that betrayals or separations will not occur.

All these structures of intensity presume or aim at order. And in the process of trying to establish family order along these lines, willful ignoring of biological or personal differences becomes necessary. Thus is the "guilt over conflict" syndrome a product of the desire for family intensity.

But suppression and avoidance of diversity along these lines is exactly of a piece with the desire for a purified, disorder-transcending identity that emerges in adolescence. The desire for coherent identity is exactly the search to avoid diversity and painful unknowns in the social arena for the sake of some secure order. What I feel sure has happened over the last decades is that intense family structure has developed as a specific mechanism for making coherent identity desires a *permanent* force in the lives of adults. This intense family configuration is the means by which adults have come to be frozen in the patterns of adolescence. The secret of these families, of their desperate longing for communion and fear of internal divergence, generating in turn all kinds of tension and hidden guilt feelings, is that they express the feelings of people still in slavery to the identity-making powers developed in their adolescence. The structures of these families, the belief that the family circle is a microcosm of the world, the belief that family members must be equals to be able to respect one another, and the terrible guilt over family conflict are specific expressions of men searching for the myth of solidarity in their lives, a solidarity born out of an inability to accept ambiguities and the painful unknown.

I have previously tried to show in a general way how

adolescent patterns might be transferred to the structure of community life. *This intense family life is the agent, the "middleman," for the infusion of adolescent fear into the social life of modern cities.* The intense family provides the materials from which the myth of common solidarity, described in the last chapter, is built. The intense family is the medium by which the whole community of families, as well as the individuals within a home, become frozen in that adolescent ritual of purifying their identities.

The transfer from family to community can be understood by the following question: is there any reason to call this kind of family structure "urban"? Could it not simply be the character of modern American family life as such, and, since most families live in urban areas, be an "urban family" trait by location only?

What contradicts such an explanation is the effect this family structure has on nonfamily social life. It is exactly the character of intense families to diminish the diversity of contact points that have marked out a community life in the teeming cities at the turn of the century. For what families of this type have done is to assign the significant social space a person perceives in the city to one special social institution, the family group. The meaning of intensity in family life is its absorbative capacity, its power to collect the interests and attention of the individual to the tight-knit band of kin. Historically, the last half-century of city life has been marked by exactly this process, a decline in the multiple contact points and associations in the city, and a rise in the number of city groups whose family life has taken on the character of what was once a family pattern for a restricted class in the city.

The sign of this absorption is contained in the most dramatic of city changes over the last, affluent decades: the growth of affluent suburbs.

The Intense Family and the New Suburbs

The classic pattern of industrial city-suburb arrangements, up to the last twenty-five years, was the pattern still extant in Turin or Paris. Cities were arranged in rings of socioeconomic wealth, with the factories at the outskirts of town, workers' suburbs or quarters next to them, and then increasingly more affluent belts of housing as one moved closer to the center of the city. There were exceptions to this pattern to be sure, but the banding seemed to apply to most of the great urban centers; in the United States, New York, Boston, and Chicago showed in general such a pattern at the opening of the present century.

In the wake of the depression and the Second World War, middle-class city dwellers in both Europe and America began a counter-urban movement of a kind not before witnessed in the history of cities. This flight to the surburbs is a complicated phenomenon that, decades later, sociologists are only beginning to grasp.

When the flight to the suburbs first began in massive numbers after the Second World War, it was commonly thought that its causes were related to the depression and to population dislocation in the war. But this explanation is simply inadequate to explain the persistence of the event over the course of time. An explanation for this suburban movement based on the economics of land is equally limited. Recent researches on choice differences between urbanite and suburbanite show that those who have moved out of the city center did so even when housing costs in city and suburb were the same for them, and even when the cost of living in the suburb was actually greater than that of living in town.

Again, in the United States, the movement to the suburbs cannot be explained by the growing presence of Negroes in the urban centers after the Second World War. For one thing, these Negroes seldom moved close to areas where young middle-class urbanites had formerly lived; for another, the lower middle-class people whose neighborhoods were gradually taken over by Negroes did not move to far-lying suburbs, but relocated only slightly farther away from the urban core. There are some exceptions to this latter pattern; there are people in outer Queens who moved to avoid blacks, but few higher up the scale living in Darien, Connecticut, who did.

The historical circumstances of depression, war, land value, and racial fear all have played a role, but they are all offshoots of a more central change in the last decades that has led to the strength of suburban life. This deeper, more hidden element is a new attitude about the conduct of family life within and without the city.

Students of modern urban life are coming to understand, still in a piecemeal way, that people who now live in suburbs value their home settings because they feel that closer family ties are more possible there than in the city center. The closeness is not so much a material one—after all, families in city apartments are extremely close physically. Rather, as is now being learned, it is the *simplification* of the social environment in the suburbs that accounts for the belief that close family life will be more possible there than in the confusion of the city.

This simplification of the social environment in suburbs is the logical end in the decline of diverse communities, discussed in the last chapter, that has occurred as people have become more affluent. For in the suburb, physical space becomes rigidly divided into functional areas: there are wide swatches of housing, separated from swatches of commercial development concentrated in that unique suburban institution, the shopping center or shopping strip; schools are similarly isolated, usually in a parklike setting. Within the housing sectors themselves, new homes have been built at homogeneous socioeconomic levels. When critics of planning reproach developers for simplifiying the environment in this way, the developers reply, truthfully, that people want to live "with people just like themselves"; people think diversity will be bad for social as well as economic reasons. The desire of people beyond the line of economic scarcity is to live in a functionally separated, internally homogeneous environment; that is the crux of the matter.

People desire this simplification because it permits the intensity of family relations to gather full force. All extraneous elements, all unknowns, or unforeseen social conditions of surprise can be minimized. This arrangement of suburban life is a means for creating that sense of long-term order and continuity on which family intensity must be based. In this way the reduction of the suburban environment to a functionally separate, internally homogeneous system permits desires for purified experience to reach their apex. The hidden assumption behind this belief is that the strength of the family bond might be weakened if the individual family members were exposed to a rich social condition, readily accessible outside the house.

When the suburbs were first taking form along these lines in the decade after World War II, some critics, like David Riesman, began to criticize them for a kind of aimlessness and emptiness in their social relations. But a hidden bond of a peculiar kind of social relations was there. It was a common determination to remain inviolate, to ensure the family's security and sanctity through exclusionary measures on race, religion, class, or other "intrusions" on a "nice community of homes." Such bonds John Seeley found in his fine study *Crestwood Heights* and Herbert Gans reveals in his recent book on the suburb of Levittown, although Gans does not interpret his findings along these lines.

' This kind of family living in the suburbs surely is a little strange. Isn't this preference for suburbia as a setting for family life in reality an admission, tacit and unspoken to be sure, that the parents do not feel confident of their own human strengths to guide the child in the midst of an environment richer and more difficult than that of the neat lawns and tidy supermarkets of the suburbs? If a close, tight-knit family emerges because the other elements of the adult and child world are made purposely weak, if parents assume their children will be better human beings for being shielded or deprived of society outside the home and homelike schools, surely the family life that results is a forced and unnatural intimacy.

Of course, there are many similar criticisms one could make of suburbs, all centered in some way on the fact that suburbanites are people who are afraid to live in a world they cannot control. This society of fear, this society willing to be dull and sterile in order that it not be confused or overwhelmed, thus shares something with the first middle-class families of the industrial city, families like those explored in my study of the Union Park neighborhood of Chicago. A fear of the richness of urban society prevails in both the early industrial city and the post-industrial suburbs of the middle class, and the family becomes a place of refuge in which the parents try to shield their children, and themselves, from the city.

However, given the processes of human development described so far in this essay, the malaise of suburban family life cuts much deeper. For these controlled communities, where people are such good friends, so carefully watching one another, are the expressions in urban terms of what a desire for purified experience can do to social life when it becomes dominant in a mass form. In the name of avoiding painful confusion, of establishing the "decencies" of life as regnant, the scope of human variety and freedom of expression is drastically restricted; this is, in broad urban terms, exactly the same pattern as is to be found in those revolutionary regimes where "the good life" is rigidly imposed as a life of discipline. The multiplicity of contact points is voluntarily reduced so that men do not lose their solidarity.

In this way intensive family life in America sapped a generation's interest in participating in dissimilar kinds of contact experiences in the city, therefore making these diverse forms of participations shrivel and lose their vitality in the last few decades. The withdrawal has been *voluntary;* it is not the result of an inevitable destruction caused by technological progress or the invasion of blacks. No mechanistic explanations are permissible that take this growth of family intensity and withdrawal from multiple contact groups out of the realm of human action. The suburban condition, which is now guiding as well the rebuilding of inner-city areas in the housing-project complexes like Lefrak City in New York, is a social creation, a social act. In that lies the great hope for rebuilding the cities, for social acts can change; they are not immutable and fixed.

The consequences of decline in wide contact points in cities can be seen most graphically in the realms of pleasure for men in cities, and the realms in which men struggle for power.

"All the Great Whorehouses Are Gone"

When I was a student living in a tenement on the south side of Chicago, one of my neighbors was a slightly tubby woman in her late thirties, who was fond of tight leopard-skin slacks, orange blouses, and slightly bluish lipstick, and who worked at night whoring. Occasionally she would have afternoon coffee at the restaurant next to our building, and we got to know each other. One of her favorite themes, expounded at great length and with a wealth of references gathered through "participant-observation," was that the whorehouse as a social institution was dying out, and that trade was forced into private apartments and losing its social character. The police were lenient, she said—that was not the problem; rather, the customers had become discomfited by the old routines of staying around for a whole evening, talking and drinking with the girls before retiring to the bedrooms. Now they wanted their sex fast and privately.

This tirade struck me as a piece of local folklore and nothing more, until I began to do some research on municipal "clean-up" campaigns on crime in the last few years. What struck me about these campaigns is that they are emotionally fed by a desire to clean up or close down a kind of vice that, as my participant observer knew, doesn't exist. "Gambling dens and whorehouses," which a few years ago were considered in some Midwestern cities the result of black urban migration, are now few and far between in cities. There is plenty of gambling, in and out of the ghettos, and some whoring, but the activities are not communalized, not intended as a social gathering. One might know a numbers man, or businessmen on trips might pick up lone girls at bars. The real crime, not touched in these emotional clean-up campaigns, centers on theft, the organized hard-drug traffic, and rackets, and to these kinds of crime the law-and-order crowd is indifferent.

But places for amusement and social contact less shady than the whorehouses or gambling rooms are also disappearing. In working-class quarters, pool halls and small bars have been rapidly on the decline. Respectable working-class men are now spending their time around the houses and yards that large numbers can now afford. The rise of affluence for these city dwellers has led directly to a new centering on home and family. Participation in church or synagogue life, as reported in the work of Will Herberg and others, is on the decline, even though many more people now formally hold church memberships. Richard Hoggarth reports a similar withdrawal from local social centers in the more affluent working-class families of Britain.

This decline has been familiar to sociologists for some time. Less familiar, but equally important, are changes in the character of amusements and social meeting grounds for the urban middle classes. Since so little is known, historically, about middle-class people in cities, what needs to be judged is the social character of a process going on right now.

In the last ten or fifteen years, small restaurants, night clubs, and bars that cater to a middle-class clientele have encountered great financial difficulties, and have been largely supplanted by enormous chain operations—like Howard Johnson's, Longchamps', or a little less fancy, the MacDonalds', groups. The small establishments find they cannot compete in volume economies and the like against these standardized giants. The same is true of the enormous hotel chains for middle-class people when they travel: it would be difficult to say what makes a Holiday Inn in Indiana different from one in New Mexico or Vermont.

The social effect of this is for middle-class people to conceive of social spaces that have a distinctive character to be intimate and small places, the most powerful being their own homes. When one wants to feel one is socializing in a personal, warm way, the downtown restaurant with a hundred tables is hardly the place; home is the place, now, where such contacts can be made. That middle-class life might be different can be seen in the style of entertaining practiced by many "old-school" middle-class families in Paris: friends can be entertained at a restaurant without discomfort, because the restaurant is usually small, and the proprietor an actual person, not a corporation with an "image." More importantly, the idea that entertaining and socializing is a public activity is accepted. Some of the Jewish delicatessens in American suburbs have this quality: one goes out to see and be seen, meets people by chance without discomfort in a public place.

But the main tendency of American middle-class socializing is the opposite; "real" entertaining is sheltered and by invitation in the private house. This is why café life, either outdoors or indoors, has failed to catch on when attempted as part of central-city urban renewal, or in the newest shopping centers. One is more "comfortable" having a cocktail at home before dinner than taking one's wife out of the house for a respite to a café or tavern.

For more affluent suburbanites, some social breaks from home occur through membership in country clubs. Social critics have been entirely too snobbish about these institutions, for they are one of the few real leverages against the intense household life of the suburbs. The difficulty with them is that they are homogeneous: by social and economic class obviously, and usually by race and religion as well. They are closed institutions, but they are at least something to widen the circle of meaningful "others" for suburban people.

These are the familiar signs of how socializing has polarized for a number of urban groups. For affluent people, public amusements have become the charge of mass, institutional businesses; the belief that the home is where personalized contacts should occur is therefore reinforced. Among working-class people of somewhat lesser means, the old neighborhood creations are dying out, in part because these "respectable" working-class families choose to spend more of their time at home. It is also true that the urban renewal of working-class neighborhoods is also destroying gathering spots. As Jane Jacobs shows, there has been destruction of arenas for social interchange—little bars, shops, and pool halls—because of a middle-class vision of what a comfortable and secure place should really be.

One can also interpret this decline of places of pleasure as a result of the "neighborhood" becoming much more definable and homogeneous in the modern city. Social scientists used to spend a great deal of time fighting with each other about the meaning of "neighborhood life" in cities, one of the principal points being that there was such a multiplicity of social contact that individuals could not be pinpointed neatly in neighborhoods. Now, I fear, they can. The growth of intensive family life, absorbing the energies of its members in the belief that the family is itself a microcosm of all there is in society, and the functional simplification of the urban environment in the suburban movement of the last quarter-century have made particular regions in the city all too identifiable in socioeconomic, racial, and functional terms. Now people really are getting to know who their neighbors are: they are just like themselves.

Arenas to Fight in

There is no more sacred shibboleth of urban reform than the cry that the bosses and the political machines of the city must go. Yet, under the impact of reform, the decline of these clubs have cut off one of the most vital contact points in the city. It may not be, as Daniel P. Moynihan once claimed, that the political machines are one of the great achievements of the modern city, but there is no denying their importance in giving individuals a connectedness to power and a forum for social as well as political exchange.

Something must first be said of the social character of political machines at the turn of the century. Often, forty or fifty years ago, these power groups had neighborhood clubhouses, where people came to meet and talk. The clubhouses were something more, as a social institution, than mere offices. And there was a sense of the closeness of help; some recent studies of Tammany Hall, for instance, show how it worked as a kind of court of last resort when people needed help. Handlin has made a similar point: the corruption and graft of these institutions was the way the goods of urban industrial society were spread down to the little man. The system of legality had to be violated if those at the bottom of the city's structure were to be "cut in" on power and its fruits.

What is important about political machines in today's cities is the way they have been fought by the virtuous and respectable orders of the city. For one sees, from the time of the Progressive Era reformers on, the urge in the clean-up campaigns to replace the personalized politics and influence peddling of the machines with routine, supposedly conflict-free bureaucratic organizations. In other words, in American cities the alternative to civic graft has been conceived essentially as the depersonalizing and routinizing of politics and political power: justice is taken to be free of personal influence and circumstance. Yet the effect of this has been a terrible paradox.

For insofar as the reform crusades have succeeded in amending the past, the little guys, the white working-class and lower middle-class voters, have lost their sense of connectedness with the body politic; when the machines lost a personalistic character, the little guys were isolated from the only channels of political influence *they* believed effective. The "alienated voter" phenomenon is not a slogan; there is, as anyone who has explored the feelings of people in ethnic neighborhoods will attest, a real and a powerful sense of disconnection. There is now a large debate going on in political science circles over whether in functional fact the little-voter is so cut off from power. From the human point of view, this debate is academic—the people themselves feel cut off, perceive themselves as robbed of something they cannot put a name to.

What they have lost results from the polarization of city life into intense families and bureaucratized structures of participation. What they have lost is an arena in the old sense of the word, a place to express themselves and fight with others in a direct way for power. The cause and its effect have an inner relationship.

For the spirit of reform is essentially a permutation of the "guilt over conflict" within the emerging families themselves. It is a belief that good relations between people are conflict-free, understandable in advance by defined rules, and stable over a long period of time. This attitude in its turn is an expression, a summation almost, of the desire for a purified identity. Reforming the corruption of the city, to the extent it has succeeded, is a brief for trying to squeeze the explosiveness out of city life by removing the elements of surprise and disorder; rules replace the vagaries of personal circumstance. But urban society becomes stratified in power relations precisely to the extent that people feel comfortable in using impersonal, bureaucratic rules as a means of achieving their ends. The upper middle classes do; the losers, the little people, do not.

As the work of Robert Lane has so incisively shown, the political competence of working-class people, white as well as black, lies in forging personal relationships and affiliations as a means for exercising power. The lower half of the city's population is, in a drive for rational reform, deprived of what it knows and understands about getting things done: the little deal, the contractor who cuts in his friends, the ward politician who calls a friend in city hall to repair a street or find a disabled constituent a nonessential job. Thus the polarization of contact groups and the congruent growth of the intimate home and the defined routines outside it create a power vacuum; the little guys in the city are deprived of a region in which to fight or cajole for what they need for themselves.

I do not intend to argue that we ought to increase graft anew, though it strikes me that a little humane graft is a good thing. But we ought to look at why machine politics came to power in the past, and salvage the good mixed in with the greed and viciousness of those regimes. To destroy the political club structures, as the middle-class reformers have succeeded in doing in many cities, simply cuts off much of the body politic from power and increases the "alienation" of these voters—hence their tendency to turn to messianic solutions from the far Right.

The New Social Space of Cities

The processes of change described in this chapter could easily be misread, along what someone has called "slum-romantic" lines. I am not arguing that we return to the old ways of city life when times were hard; rather, I have tried to show how the emergence of a new city life in an era of abundance and prosperity has eclipsed something of the essence of urban life—its diversity and possibilities for complex experience. What needs to happen is a change in the peculiar institutions of affluent city life, in order to create new forms of complexity and new forms of diverse experience.

It is common for "slum romantics" to bemoan the loss of intimate social space and small scale in modern city life. But from the vantage point of what has been set forth here, the issue would appear to be the reverse. There has not been a loss of intimate small scale, per se, but rather a loss of multiple foci of small scale. The urban family of this affluent era has developed a power to absorb activities and interests that were once played out in a variety of settings in the city. Indeed, it might best be said of city life during the past twenty-five years of suburban growth that the scale of life has become too intimate, too intense.

For it is out of the ordering patterns of this new intensity that the evils of purified community life can arise. It is the polarization of intimacy that permits withdrawal from active participation in unknown social situations in the city: after all, why venture beyond home, since it is a mirror of all that lies beyond? It is this same inner-turning little world that, unused to the daily shocks of confrontation and the expression of ineradicable conflict, reacts with such volatility to the disorders of oppressed groups in the city, and meets the hostility from below with an oppressive hand greatly out of proportion to the original challenges.

Most important, this new configuration of polarized intimacy in the city provides the individual with a powerful moral tool in shutting out new or unknown social relations for himself. For if the suburbanized family is a little world of its own, and if the dignity of that family consists in creating bases of long-term stability and trust, then potentially diversifying experiences can be shut out with the feeling of performing a moral act. For the sake of "protecting the home" a man refuses to wander or explore; this is the meaning of that curious self-satisfaction men derive in explaining what they gave up "for the sake of the children." It is to make impotence a virtue.

In these ways, the polarization of contact groups in the development of cities during the age of affluence has created a generation of adult puritans. The new virtue, like the religious puritanism of old, is a ritual of purifying the self of diverse and conflicting avenues of experience. But where the first puritans engaged in this self-repression for the greater glory of God, the puritans of today repress themselves out of fear, fear of the unknown, the uncontrolled. The intense family is the *via regia* by which this fear is maintained; such a family makes out of even men's intimate lives a known function. Given this transformation of the family, the less intimate social relations in cities have also had to change. The material abundance in the modern city has been manipulated to make suburbanized space, in new inner-city housing as well as in the suburbs themselves, space that is purified to a brutal and functional simplicity.

I believe we can learn to put the material wealth in city life to use as an agent of freedom, rather than voluntary slavery. But to do so we shall have to reverse a complimentary pattern of withdrawal from complexity that has grown up in the professionalized shaping of urban places by city planners.

CHAPTER FOUR

Planning
Purified Cities

THE TERRAIN EXPLORED THUS FAR REVEALS A NEW MAN living in a new community: a secular puritan, afraid of his own powers to explore what he cannot control in advance; a community life whose institutions, notably the family, encourage his puritanism to become a permanent way of life. This new breed of puritan has succeeded in making the social framework of his existence increasingly simpler and more primitive. Yet the brutality of his impulses has occurred in the midst of a great flowering of technology and mechanical invention.

The increase of technological complexity in modern society and the decrease of complexity in its social forms have not proceeded on wholly disparate planes. The impact of technological processes on community life has come to center on an area that at first glance may seen remote. This realm is a group of assumptions by which professional planners conceive and mold cities. Indeed, to make better communal use of the techology that has created abundance, we shall need to reverse certain technological assumptions about building massive cities. These assumptions were first dramatized in Paris a hundred years ago, and are now widespread throughout most of western Europe and the United States. This century of city building has, in Lewis Mumford's phrase, confused a machine-using society with a vision of society as a machine itself. Until the peculiar calculus of efficiency guiding much of city planning is united with a new conception of the humane uses of cities, I am convinced planners will create urban conditions that intensify purity drives and so promote voluntary withdrawal from social participation and the willingness to use violence as a final solution.

Let me be clear at the outset that I am not arguing that we abandon the current technological approach in favor of an opposite group of "human values," because tools are human creations themselves, and not alien in their own right. Indeed, it is now very unfortunate that the critics of present planning assumptions can only follow the vision of Camillo Sitte a century ago; modern critics still dream his dream of a return to some Arcadian, pre-industrial order where the division of labor is muted. The answer to technological problems and rigidities has all too often been an argument for a willful simplicity of urban life, as though men could put their powers to create out of mind. I believe with Lewis Mumford that it is necessary to learn to use tools in humane ways, not abandon them in order to be humane. The task is to find out what the right social ends are for the vast advances in city-building, in engineering, housing, sanitation, and road construction during the past century.

Baron Haussmann's Dream

City planning by specialists is a recent event in the history of cities. The reason for this is largely that, up to the time of the great industrial cities, urban society was not thought to be a special kind of social order. Earlier social theorists recognized in specific matters many differences between country and town. But even in Renaissance cities, writers like Machiavelli did not believe city society was subject to different rules and had a basically different set, or ordering, of social principles. For example, the special freedom of most pre-industrial city men from serfdom was not taken to bear on the general nature of "freedom in society." The city was not accorded the importance of such a special form; it was viewed instead as a fragment of a larger design. Thus the leaders of urban society were not special men of the city; rather, they were popes like Sixtus V, or monarchs like Louis XIV, who built the last of the imperial cities (for Versailles truly was such a place, not an anti-city as some have called it).

But the economic order that began to coalesce in cities about 150 years ago changed social thinkers' conception of cities. What happened was that cities lost their older shape, and so men began to wonder about what was peculiar to them in the first place. For one thing, the technological and capital-forming processes of the industrial metropolis were not subject to the kinds of power control that had operated in the cities of the past; the origin of these two processes lay beyond the older regulatory rules of cities or city states. It would have been meaningless for one city government alone to choose railroads over ships as the commerce medium of the city: the balance of trade was not to be controlled so locally. The process of industrial capital formation was in this way different from the capital formation process inspired by voyages of trade and exploration, such as those sponsored in the Renaissance by cities like Venice. Again, the ideological beliefs of men of John Stuart Mill's generation preached that these new industrial forces would of themselves operate to the benefit of all men, if only allowed to work unhampered by other political (or emotional, or historical) considerations.

Therefore, as industrial cities grew in population and economic importance, they came to be more uncontrolled, and rules of social welfare lost their historical power. We know now the evils of this transformation—the intense poverty, the uncertainty of health and vocation, the unending boredom of the physical appearance of these cities; so did the more enlightened men of the nineteenth century. It is to one such man, Baron Haussmann, that we owe the impetus to urban reform that has come to dominate our own era.

Haussmann was a man of modest background but

grand ideas who directed, at the bidding of Napoleon the Third, the rebuilding of the city of Paris in the 1860's. Paris at this time was a mosaic of the industrial and the pre-industrial orders. New factories were growing rapidly on the outskirts of the city and in certain sections of the inner city as well; but the tangle of small crooked streets and decaying buildings was still the focus for economic activities new and old, with a populace increasingly unknown to the administrative and social-service authorities of the city. Movement within the city itself was very difficult—in 1840 it took an hour and a half to walk on foot between two sections of Paris; the distance can now be navigated on foot in thirty minutes. Especially frightening to the political authorities was the fact there was no way of controlling the workers in case of civil insurrection, since the twisted streets were perfect for setting up impromptu barricades.

Haussmann's means of correcting the wretched housing, the difficult transport, the lack of political control are important to us now because he was the first to look on the solution of these problems as essentially interrelated. What one did with transport could also be a means of dealing with the populace when civil disorders occurred; how one removed the dilapidated housing, Haussmann believed, was also a way of defining the relations between the social classes.

Haussmann began to cut, through the jumble of streets, great, long, unswervingly straight avenues, avenues that could accommodate an enormous amount of traffic, serve as an easy means of getting troops into riotous sections of the city, and act like river boundaries dividing different socioeconomic sections of the city. They were put in relation to the city's institutions along lines first laid down in the great Baroque era of city planning in the sixteen and early seventeenth centuries. These broad avenues connected public monument to public monument; they did not connect one group of people to another with whom they might have social relations. The working man's districts of Paris thus remained, in the wake of Haussmann's reforms, unconnected to the new centers of industry on the outskirts of town. Again, these new streets often served to put the purely social problems of poverty and petit-bourgeois deprivation out of mind by putting them out of sight behind the beautiful grand boulevards.

Baron Haussmann was, to be sure, a great creator, and his positive accomplishments cannot be ignored. Yet his legacy to the cities of our time, unintended or not, has been a group of assumptions of terrible simplicity.

The first of these is that it is desirable to treat city problems as a whole: this belief rather thoughtlessly assumes that because the social, economic, and physical phenomena of a city are interrelated in their functioning, it is a good idea to try to deal with them in a coherent way, so that changes in one realm will inevitably transform other realms of city life in structured paths.

The second assumption is that it is a good idea to plan physical space for predetermined social use; that is, instead of assuming that changes in the social structure of the city should be accomplished first in order to change the physical appearance of the city, Haussmann bequeathed the notion to us that it is somehow better, and certainly easier, to change the physical landscape in order to alter the social patterns of the metropolis.

These ideas seem now so routine as to appear self-evident common sense. Yet they are not ineluctable rules, but in fact the product of a peculiar historical response men have made to their own capacity to live with the machines and technological artifacts on which the modern bureaucratic order, whether capitalist or state socialist, is built. This peculiar historical response can best be understood by looking at the transmutation—or better, the intensification—of Haussmann's beliefs in the major planning movement of this century, the metropolitan-regional planning movement.

The Great Plans

By the beginning of the Second World War, those concerned with the organization of cities had, by and large, become ideologues of a peculiar sort. Their dogma was hardly an emotional one, nor an ideal of great intellectual depth, but these deficiencies were more than compensated for by a doglike faith in what has come to be called "metropolitan planning." This planning ideal, which gathered strength in the 1930's—although it was contained in germ in the writings of Ebenezer Howard at the turn of the century—proposed to take the assumptions behind Haussmann's rebuilding of Paris one step further: city planners would design coherently the growth of whole urban regions, coordinate the physical, economic, and social efforts not only within the jurisdiction of one city, but also in relation to the needs of other cities around it. What was in Haussmann's work an assumption of the desirable power of one part of the urban complex to affect other parts became in the metropolitan planning ideology an ideal of *planning the parts from the nature of the whole.*

This is of course one of the most familiar modern images of unity: it is the basis on which machines are designed and it defines a peculiarly modern concept of "efficiency" in technological and social organization. But, as historians like John Nef have gone to great efforts to show, this image is an assumption about efficiency rather than the nature of efficiency itself. In pre-industrial factory systems, the experience of making a product was more important than a standard image, a clear picture, of the "whole" to be made; those craftsmen conceived, therefore, that to define in advance what a thing should look like would interfere with "efficiency," that is, with the freedom of the craftsmen to exploit his materials and forms during production. In an industrial situation, the product to be made is conceived beforehand, so that the realization of the product, the achievement of the whole, is a passive routine, not an active experience or exploration. By envisioning the fruit of labor in advance of labor itself it is therefore possible to plan the production process so that the "parts are determined by the whole," since the parts of production are thought to have no life of their own, no role other than to work harmoniously toward the creation of a preplanned entity.

This mentality of production obviously suits, even invites, the use of machine tools instead of human labor. Indeed, given this idea, one of the great humane accomplishments of the technology of the last three decades has been to automate such production devices as the assembly line, where men used to perform labor that was not suited to their capacity to experience newness and variety. Yet when this mentality of production, this image of machine efficiency, becomes transferred to the production of cities, in the designing of social parts from a predetermined, pre-visualized urban whole, the results become inhumane.

In planning done along this line, the planner first determines the "projective needs" of an urban area in the present and future, and then proceeds to design the physical and social facilities, the "parts," to service them. The assumption is that the larger the scale of this process, the more efficient, in the machine sense, the results. In a recent, widely praised collection of essays on planning, the editor concludes, for example:

> . . . the amount of area covered by plans should be continually enlarged. There is a distinct need for a national urbanization pattern or locational strategy for the entire United States; moreover, this should be co-ordinated with Canada and Mexico on the continental level.[1]

If such massive coordination were to succeed, the same writer believes, then it would be necessary to preplan all

[1] W. Wentworth Eldridge, ed.: *Taming Megalopolis* (Garden City, N.Y.: Anchor Books; 1967), p. 1158.

aspects of social and economic life in relation to each other. This "unified approach" entails the following:

> Aesthetic and humanistic values and institutions must be in a planned relationship to economic and political values and institutions. Thus all such activities must be designed as a unit both physically and as social structures. Clearly both the public and the private structures must be meshed.[2]

These are not the words of a mad superman. They are rather a clear statement of the goals of a large and influential segment of the profession that plans modern cities. The ideal is that nothing be out of control. For life to be manipulated on so tight a rein, all manner of diverse activities must be ruled by their lowest common denominators. The result of planning efforts along these lines is that the future environment becomes a function of the planner's vision of it in the present, just as the machine is the product of the machine's designer, and not its fabricator. Thus, the inhabitants of future urban spaces do not possess them of their own making, as for example the people of Jewish ghettos in central Europe gradually possessed the neighborhoods they came to live in. That historical process is replaced by an arbitrary assignment of who is suited to live where.

In the beginning of this book it was shown how the device of "projected needs" was a ruse to avoid facing the unknown in the future. What is peculiarly mechanical about this approach to time is that a majority of the

[2] Ibid.

planners proceeding on these lines conceive of the "needs" of urbanites not in terms of known experience, but rather in terms of the urbanites' place in an order where needs are experienced abstractly, as part of a total function. To the arguments of those displaced by highway-building or urban renewal projects, the planners respond that they work in terms of an urban whole, but this metropolitan region is itself a "community" only as the functioning parts of a machine could be called a "community."

Thus Haussmann's first precept, that the changes in one urban sphere of activity should change other spheres of activity, becomes transmuted into the concept that the significant functioning of the city itself is found in the links between specific activities in the city. It is not what people do or experience in their own lives that counts, but the external relationship of these acts to areas of indirect experience that is the focus. Now, no one could argue with metropolitan planners that these external relationships, these interstices, exist and that they do shape certain large relationships in the city. The question is, why adopt them as the important focus? Why single out the fact of their existence as the desirable value? That the functioning of the whole to its peak efficiency is the best means of life for the parts holds in the design of machines, but how can it be justified in the affairs of men? If anything, men should be encouraged to strike out from the paths of easiest resistance in dealing with each other, encouraged to form relationships that have a different pattern and direction from those that have existed before: this is how the phenomenon of history distinguishes men from other kinds of animals.

✳ The "Urban Whole" as a Myth of Purity

Why progressive notions of city planning have taken on this tone has to do, as was suggested at the opening of this book, with what planners feel about the complexity possible in city life. Their impulse has been to give way to that tendency, developed in adolescence, of men to control unknown threats by eliminating the possibility for experiencing surprise. By controlling the frame of what is available for social interaction, the subsequent path of social action is tamed. Social history is replaced by the passive "product" of social planning. Buried in this hunger for preplanning along machinelike lines is the desire to avoid pain, to create a transcendent order of living that is immune to the variety, and so to the inevitable conflict, between men. Let us see why this is so.

The metaphor of metropolitan planning is an expression of the technology by which modern machines are constructed. The parts of machines are different, to be sure, but these differences exist to create a single function; any conflict between the parts, or even the existence of parts working independently of the whole, would defeat the purpose of the machine. There is no reason for pain or confusion in it.

But when this metaphor from technology is used for the structure of urban society, its meaning changes. Here the technological metaphor of city growth defeats the needs for which the whole exists, because these needs reside in the human parts of the social whole, not in some social product apart from social experience. In planning cities on the machine model, an urbanist is trying to "integrate" these needs in a transcendent way, and for the purposes of this integration conflict and pain between the parts of the human city are viewed as bad, as qualities to be eliminated. This is the same spirit as that found in excessive post-revolutionary discipline, or in the flight to hiding in a clean suburb. The actual, immediate experience of man, in all its possible freedom and diversity, is taken to be less important than the creation of a community that is conflict free; the sense of living in the present is violated for an ideal society in which men live in such harmony that one can never imagine them growing in ways that will violate the "correct" interrelations they have with each other.

Thus does the technological imagery of metropolitan planning lead to an adolescent society, as easily as the isolated little suburbs do. It is rare that city planning under this guise should even contemplate, much less encourage, the development of social situations that might lead to communal tension through the encouragement of human differences. Conflict is conceived as a threat to some "better," conflict-free city life. And when conflict in the cities comes, no conception even exists among the professional planners as to how conflicts can be expressed fully without leading to violence. Because the metropolitan planning persuasion is so naïve in its assumptions of what constitutes the good city, because it is an expression of adolescent refusal to deal with the world in all its complexity and pain, the escalation of urban conflict into violence must inevitably result, for the planners are not really concerned with mediating actual human behavior or providing fields of unpredictable interaction. The essence of the purification mechanism is a fear of losing control. Real disorder is a problem, planners think, best left to politicians and the like. Planners' sights are on that urban "whole" instead; they are dreaming of a beautiful city that exists somewhere other than in the present, a beautiful city where people fit together in peace and harmony, a city so beautiful in fact, that ghetto people, Irish cops, aristocratic WASPS, hippies, students, clerks, and bookkeepers will close their eyes to what they cannot abide in each other, to the painful facts of their difference, and settle down to common happiness.

There is a hidden dimension to this metropolitan ideal. In the communities organized around coherence Tocqueville viewed, the effect of forming a communal image of solidarity was to free the individuals of the community from the need to confront and interact with each other directly. In the idealization of coherence made by the professional planners of cities, there occurs a similar disengagement. From the vantage point of leadership in city affairs, however, this disengagement leads to a failure in effectiveness, an impotence to achieve what the planners want for themselves. The very nature of the technological metaphor involved in holistic planning creates this impotence. For machines do not change their output by spontaneous changes in their parts, except to break down. When a machine's parts wear down, which is their "form of experience" in time, the machine cannot operate. But the essence of human development is that *growth* occurs when old routines break down, when old parts are no longer enough for the needs of the new organism. This same kind of change, in a larger sphere, creates the phenomenon of history in a culture.

To put the matter more concretely: today plans or "master guides" are made for whole metropolitan regions. Planners try to guide the history of their cities' future according to predetermined, specified lines; some parts of the plan when realized evolve historically to conflict with the others; it is then thought that the plan has failed. The "whole" has fallen apart, for it is not conceived of being able to grow in unknown ways. Growth, in massive planning, is instead conceived along mechanical lines as the realization of an initial vision. This has been the inner contradiction that has crippled the very act of planning for large cities; there is no provision for the fact of history, for the unintended, for the contradictory, for the unknown.

In his penetrating and unfairly neglected book *The Last Landscape*, William H. Whyte has shown the impotence of planners working along these lines in their attempts to structure the Washington, D.C., urban region. The planners imposed an ideal image of urban growth on the city that the facts of city history are now violating; new residential and commercial growth is occurring in areas where the planners had not expected the city to grow; the central city is renewing itself in ways not originally anticipated. The response of the planners, as Whyte shows, has not been to try to understand the new changes and learn from them, but rather to cry for greater policing powers to enforce what they originally envisioned. Failing to get these powers, there has now developed a resigned passivity among the original planners: what can they do if they cannot be "in control"? Precisely because the massive planning ideal is resistant in its intentions to the idea of history in a city's life, the planners are bound always in the end to be out of control. In this way, there has developed, internally, a vacuum in professional leadership in cities.

An obvious, painfully obvious, result of this vacuum is what has happened in large cities of America and western Europe in the planning of highways. Here, certainly, the funds and governmental power to plan, through Port and Interstate authorities, have not been absent; if anything, these programs in American cities have had almost tyrannical power in enforcing their ideas. Yet they have failed, not for lack of technological expertise, but because they have not had the power to be adaptive over the course of time: no provisions have been made for the interaction of traffic design in cities with the changing character of the inner city itself. The planners did not envision an environment different from what was conceived in the "planning stages"; but, as the roads were built, more people decided to use their cars and there were more people with cars to use. And so the traffic jams remain as bad as they were before the new highways were built, only on a more massive scale. The fault here is not that the planners failed to be omniscient, but that they presumed themselves omniscient before they built, and so made no provisions for considering change and evolution in their designs, or even whether their original ideas were worth pursuing, in the course of realizing the large-scale and long-term plans.

Humanists often despair before what they imagine to

be the unconquerable power of technological forces. But technological patterns, like anything that grows out of a specific historical situation, have controlling power over only the forces related to their own growth. Since the growth of machine technology was *not* generated by social forces directly related to urban social structure, its re-imposition on the city is bound to lead to the kind of breakdowns we are now experiencing in transportation, public and publicly directed rehousing, and the like. In the shaping of cities, the technological metaphor is not practical; it simply doesn't work.

As for the human "parts" involved, the writings of such urbanists as Charles Abrams, Jane Jacobs, Marc Fried, and Herbert Gans have by now made us painfully aware of how much is destroyed in the lives of real people for the sake of realizing some abstract plan of development or renewal.

Fried, for example, in his superb essay "Grieving for a Lost Home" has documented the feeling of sudden empti-ness among a group of ordinary city dwellers who were moved from a decayed area slated for urban renewal into clean, modern, preplanned housing elsewhere in the city. Suddenly people who had developed neighborly contacts, day-to-day associations and loyalties, found themselves scattered and alone like refugees, as a result of change made "for their own good." The planners' response to this kind of complaint has been that any social change involves dislocation to someone. True enough, but then who would the planners point to as the ultimate recipients of the changes they propose? Certainly not the suburbanites— what they want, and get, is insulation from the urban region as a totality; again, the results of a wide range of recent research on lower middle-class and lower-class people who have been shifted from their old living areas into the new, preplanned communities reveal this same "grieving" Fried has depicted. The studies hardly indicate a wild enthusiasm on the part of ordinary city dwellers for their new place in the grand scheme.

It is not enough for city planners to argue that they provide the technological materials for social life and that the responsibility for how the materials are used rests with the people in the city. This argument is one that natural scientists have come to treat with great suspicion among themselves. The contemporary scientific community in the last decades has come to see that nothing invented by man can be divorced from human use; there are no humanly "neutral" acts of creation or invention, no matter how detached or objective the scientist feels in his work. This is the lesson the planning community now needs to learn: it must take responsibility for its acts in a historical, unpredictable society rather than in a dream world of harmony and predetermined order.

To make modern cities serve human needs, we shall have to change the way in which city planners work. Instead of planning for some abstract urban whole, planners are going to have to work for the concrete parts of the city, the different classes, ethnic groups, and races it contains. And the work they do for these people cannot be laying out their future; the people will have no chance to mature unless they do that for themselves, unless they are actively involved in shaping their social lives. But because the needs of life are not shapeless, because there is a substance of growth, and not an aimless wandering, planners can provide the social materials by which men in communities can come to civilize themselves.

This is a more complex notion than it might appear at first. Unlike many community workers who think of themselves as New Left, I cannot believe that whatever a community does by itself is *per se* good because it was self-instituted; people can want to be vicious together, like the German Nazis, or the groups of white crackers who terrorized Negroes in the old South. The impulse to create a communal order of a repressive kind rises *naturally* out of men's lives. But, out of the same complex desires for a mythic community solidarity, men can never become good simply by following the good orders or good plan of someone else; the first chapters of this book showed why that is so, I hope, from a psychological point of view. In between aimless wandering of communal life and the authoritarian direction of the community stands a middle way, which is not a compromise between the two extremes, but an entirely new approach. This new kind of city planning could create the materials human beings need, from the world outside themselves, to grow out of those peculiar modes of retreating from new and unknown experience learned on the eve of adulthood.

PART TWO

A New Anarchism

Introduction to Part Two

It is hard to think about urban social change that is not addressed to poverty. Yet the purification patterns sketched so far show a deep and convoluted sickness in the community life of city dwellers who are not poor. This is an emotional poverty rather than material poverty, and it is voluntary. In that fact lie both a reason and a hope for change.

In the writings of Herbert Marcuse and Norman O. Brown there is a pessimism, an undercurrent of despair about the social consequences of abundance. The traits of community life that Marcuse and Brown describe are in some ways similar to the picture I have drawn: a "one-dimensionality," as Marcuse calls it, in what men have made of their lives. And yet my thinking diverges sharply from Marcuse's in that this emotional poverty I take to be "caused" by something basic to the growing process of the human being himself: abundance in urban community life has only made it possible for this deep-down passion for slavery to express itself. It is too easy to lay the root of such troubles at the impersonal, mechanical schemes that have created the economic frame, the abundance of the age. What the past decades have taught us is not how rotten abundance as such is, but how rotten are the uses to which it is put.

If change in the social uses of abundance is to occur, the psychological forces of adult life need to be balanced in a new way. To make good use of affluence, we must create a set of social situations that will weaken, as a man matures, the desire for controlled, purified experience. Perhaps I have more faith than Marcuse that a change can occur, since the origin of these communal ills seems to me to spring from a freeze or arrest in the development of most men, now, in the problems of their adolescence. For there is a *possible* adulthood that lies beyond this adolescence. If that adulthood were brought into being, then, I believe, the slaveries to which affluent community life is now subject could end, and the abundance used to enrich man's freedom.

The terms of this possible adulthood may already be evident: a life with other people in which men learn to tolerate painful ambiguity and uncertainty. To counter the desire for slavery that grows strong in adolescence, men must subsequently grow to need the unknown, to feel incomplete without a certain anarchy in their lives, to learn, as Denis de Rougemont says, to love the "otherness" around them.

This may seem far from the experiences of social life men now have in cities, yet I believe the city will play a vital role in encouraging a move into this new adulthood. For if the multiple points of social contact once characterizing the city can be reawakened under terms appropriate to affluence, then some channels for experiencing diversity and disorder will again be open to men. The great promise of city life is a new kind of confusion possible within its borders, an anarchy that will not destroy men, but make them richer and more mature.

CHAPTER FIVE

Outgrowing a Purified Identity

HOW DO MEN LEARN TO ACCEPT PAINFUL SURPRISES AND disorder? In that acceptance lies the secret of how purification myths come to seem unreal. Since the myths take on full force in the crisis of adolescence, the process of learning to face pain tells something as well about how adolescence is transcended and adulthood gained.

An easy cliché has it that suffering makes men's lives "meaningful." We know that men who take the exit into permanent psychosis suffer terribly; whole communities of men also suffer, from hunger, from slavery. It seems a paltry thing to say these lives are therefore meaningful, the suffering productive. Indeed, the surest way to acquire a sympathy for the revolutionaries of the nineteenth century is to read various ministers' tracts for the poor, in which fourteen hours a day of heavy labor are described as a "blessing given to discipline lust and the passions of the flesh." The modern equivalent of this stupidity is that which says the black people will grow stronger through their need to struggle, as though the elementary decencies of life, effortlessly accorded the majority, were so precious that the minority should go through a hellish test to be worthy to possess them.

It is grotesque to look on misery as a blessing; yet I would argue as well that the visions of society without pain can never be; in fact, such visions now often lead revolutionary leaders to create what their ideologies abhor, even more pain and oppression in the world. This is but another facet of the same slavery under the guise of "decency," of self-restrictive solidarity. Thus, great injustice seems to arise when a certain pain and disorder in social life is consciously avoided.

The experience of certain young revolutionary leaders suggests a way exceptionally strong men have worked beyond this paradox. It sometimes occurs that when outbreaks by the young fail in the first attempt, a deep change occurs in the lives of certain leaders; these men grow stronger in their commitment to the cause, yet the nature of the commitment is transformed by the experience of failure. The Russians Borodin and Garine, who were active in the Chinese Revolution, exemplify this change: they experienced in themselves a certain loss of systematic approach and an absorption in details that do not follow directly from revolutionary doctrine, although their faith in that doctrine remained strong. The same shift occurred for a few of the students involved in the college disorders of 1968–9. The crushing of their efforts did not blunt the desire for change, but they became more curious about their enemies and themselves apart from the struggle for power; the failure made them live more in terms of understanding those who are different.

What happened to these exceptional young people was that they abandoned the self-enclosing purity of someone like Hong, Malraux's youthful character in *The Conquerors*. These young people came to have a curiosity about the immediate world around them, a concern about their enemies as well as about themselves. This occurred, I am convinced, because something innate to the child, which languished during adolescence, was revived by their *failure* to conquer the outside world. Because they failed, their childhood curiosity was renewed about things and people in the immediate world, a world too large to control coherently. In certain circles now, for instance, one finds a compassion for the police, a desire to know how their lives have come to make them detest the students and the blacks.

What is so subtle about the changes in such young people is that their commitment has remained strong. Only now, as the result of a failure the first time in acting out revolutionary ideas, the revolutionary commitment coexists with a new desire to see, to touch, to understand, apart from the preordained truths of a coherent ideology. This compassion for the enemies—the police, the white factory workers who hate them, even for the middle-class parents—produced among these exceptional people a humility and willingness to be self-critical. That is the hidden story of much of what occurred in the last year (hidden because the press, in search of easy pictures of "them" and "us," probed only the degrees of radical commitment, and not the experience of the commitment itself in this generation).

This conversion process, which admittedly touched the lives of only an exceptional minority of student "rebels," shows how a certain kind of failure weakened the myths of a purified "us" and "them." The response to failure among these young people was peculiar, however, and sets them off as strong people. A characteristic other than the supposedly extreme nature of their ideology made them exceptional.

Every young man, on the eve of his adulthood, has dreams for himself, dreams about what he wants to do, to find out, to accomplish. These dreams for the future are the heart of how he conceives of his identity; as has been shown, these dreams tend to cohere in one solidified picture because the young man finds it hard to live with ambiguities or dissonance. But everyone dreams beyond his power. In the course of adulthood not all these youthful desires will be realized, and a man will be forced to salvage what pleasure he can in the midst of frustration. What happens to most adults, which did not happen to some of the young radicals during recent events, is that the failure makes them feel the dreams were no good; subsequently, most adults await whatever routine is dealt them. The difficulty now is that unexceptional adults believe the loss of youthful dreaming is itself "growing up," as though adulthood were the passive conclusion to a doomed activity and hope during adolescence.

But this movement from dreaming, on the one hand, to

passively going through the available routines, on the other, is not a breaking apart of the purification patterns. It is just this passive resignation which is so easy, which allows a man to sink into comfortable patterns of no challenge, and so prolong the worst strength of his adolescence, the strength to avoid having to act in unknown, not easily controllable situations. The fear of the unknown that caused the youth to dream a life for himself in which everything fit together is transmuted in adulthood into a fear of acting outside mechanical paths because the first dreams could not come true. "Giving up" is a very common way affluent adults describe the tenor of their adulthood; social studies show this true for a much wider range of people than those with severe depression disorders. But "giving up" is a comfortable act, and men who have done so can unite to put down the challengers of their routine and their peace. What is to be learned from exceptional people like the young radicals I have described is not an ideology but the reason why they accepted the fact that their first dreams failed and yet held onto the fact of belief. What needs to be found in affluent community life are the means by which such a strength can be encouraged in everyday life.

Breaking Apart the Need for a Purified Identity

There is a four-stage process, as I conceive it, in the movement from the adolescent strength, in which young people piece together an identity where everything fits, to the strength in adulthood of accepting as real dissonant and painfully conflicting experiences.

Stage One: Adolescence brings to a head the imbalance between the capacity for experience and the fund of experience available that could guide new powers and strengths. The human being is able to replace his parents at the very heart of what before constituted their authority, for he is able to synthesize moral and value rules that define his identity in a social context wider than the family.

Stage Two: The tension in this growth imbalance can be resolved through the mechanisms of purified experience in creating an identity, so that the individual projects the meaning of experiences he is afraid to have, and thus seals himself off from actually confronting the unknown in the social world around him. The coherent identity that emerges leads to a voluntary limitation and withdrawal in social life, a servitude to projections of social reality that are unified and pain-transcending.

These two stages of development, I believe, mark the character of change in a large number of lives now. As the first chapters of this book have tried to show, the social institutions of the modern city encourage growth to be frozen in this way, so that hiding from the unknown is carried into adult social life as a means of establishing a feeling of "community" in unthreatening sameness.

It is this normal adulthood pattern which must be broken. The experience of some exceptionally strong youthful revolutionaries hints at what could evolve.

Stage Three: In trying to enforce a vision of coherent order, the young person meets an immovable obstacle or social situation that is out of his control. The disorderly world defeats the dreams of coherence and solidarity.

How the defeat occurs is crucial. When the dreams of the more idealistic young—which is to say, a large number of young people—are simply ignored, or rejected through coercive force, nothing is changed. What those who now deploy the police or the school administrations against idealistic young people fail to see is that the policemen's clubs do not destroy; they vindicate the truth of the adolescent challenge thrown down. What collapsed, in a good way, during the rebellions of 1968 was rather the assumption that "we," the students, are good, "they," the establishment, are bad. These purified images collapsed and a compassion was born. That hidden productive failure had nothing to do with police. If purified identity images can be broken because the individual *feels* them unreal for the present moment and its demands, if somehow he can be brought to understanding that failure, what could be the possible result?

Stage Four: Childhood curiosity about the immediate world is reborn. The desire to see, apart from the desire to see things in their proper place, is regenerated. In other words, the courage to look in unknown places and experience feelings and situations one has not met before re-emerges. And out of this process can come a kind of human concern centered on and appreciative of the "otherness" in the world.

These stages of development summarize complex growth patterns in perhaps too sweeping a fashion. To reveal the complexity it is easiest to look at the end point of these four stages, the opposition to adolescent purification desires. I have spoken of this state as a *possible* adulthood, but something more than just its logical outlines can be seen. For the case histories of successful treatment of certain mental disorders—notably schizophrenic disturbances where a large degree of hysteria is present—reveal the characteristics of adult identity freed from this need for purified experience. Just as psychologists have interpreted purification desires in an extreme form as individual "pathology," the treatment of such pathological individuals may show how the pathology in its social form may be treated as well.

Contrasts of Adulthood to Adolescent Identity: The Loss of Omnipotence

When a man's vision of order, of a pure and painless life, has been defeated by a social world too complex to be disciplined, the man isn't defeated, only his belief in his own omnipotence is. For the purification urge is precisely the desire to be all-powerful, to control the meanings of experience before encounter so as not to be overwhelmed. As Heinz Hartmann has observed, however, losing the feeling of being omnipotent is the birth of feeling personally strong in another way.

This new sense of personal power has been termed, in

the literature of one branch of psychoanalysis, a fully developed "ego strength." What is meant by the jargon is that although an adult feels no longer wholly the manipulator of the world around him he also feels that that world cannot in turn wholly manipulate him. A certain kind of self-sufficient aloneness and singleness is born, paradoxically, at the moment when a man sees he is not going to be able to be the master of all that occurs in his life. This has been expressed by religious writers like Martin Buber as the feeling that once a man sees himself as "one among many" rather than as the master and therefore the mirror of the social world, the sense of his "being greater than his attributes" is born. The idea of ego strength tries to describe this feeling on a less mystical plane: a certain strength is affirmed through shedding the belief in the masterful power of the self.

What is meant psychologically by this strength can be shown in two ways. In clinical work with hysterical individuals, therapists have observed the hysteria to be a controlling device: if social situations are charged up to the level of hysterical emotion, the person feeling hysterical can be in total control. He or she, after all, is the one making them hysterical in character. Hysteria is therefore often interpreted as a fear of what will happen were a person not absolutely in control of the surrounding world. In therapy with such people, the goal becomes one of convincing them that they have a strength and an inner being apart from their ability to control the environment. When the therapy works, there seems to be kindled a great sense of strength in the patient, not only in the freedom from the hysteria, but also in a feeling that the patient will not be destroyed by new wandering or exploring.

A second way of understanding this ego strength that comes from feeling limited is in terms of the concept of identity itself. In the strict sense of the term used by Erikson and Hartmann, identity is a conscious way of forming the rules by which one places oneself in social space—it is precisely an identifying of oneself in society. Coherent identity patterns that emerge in adolescence are a way of *identifying* oneself as a controller; when coherence patterns are broken, one identifies oneself as a being in the midst of other beings: one can influence them but not make them over in one's own image. Conversely there is something in oneself they cannot make over.

That something is a different kind of identity-making process, for adult identity comes to be defined as a set of *acts* that a person can perform rather than a set of *attributes* or possessed characteristics. The difference is critical. The self-images developed in adolescence are what Peter Blos calls objects of self-hood, static symbols or beliefs that identify who the adolescent is within the circles he moves in. In the possible adulthood that lies beyond adolescence, the need to label one's identity by what one possesses or what one thinks bows to a sense of self-hood created by virtue of a certain kind of action. In order to perform this action a man must learn the futility of trying to fix immutably his relation to his social world through symbols or attributes of identity. This act I call caring.

Caring: The Consequence of Being Limited

Something happens to the quality of a person's concern when he loses the adolescent desire to be omnipotent. The change is embodied by two alternative uses of the word "caring."

In everyday language, we speak of "caring about" someone, and also of "caring for" someone. When we say we care for someone, we mean something stronger than the first expression; we almost mean at times that we want to take care of them. This in turn psychologically works so that we will take them over, that they might drown in us. This is one way of looking at strength in a relationship between two people in love.

Therapists have found, in looking at marriage patterns of schizophrenics, that this sort of caring creates something evil between husband and wife. This form of caring becomes a drive for power and a demonstration of prowess. In a social realm, the same kind of caring is perhaps what underlies Weber's notion of charisma, for it is at the heart of the desire to lead, and also the urge to be led. The latter—to be led under the guise of being cared for—is the more frightening, in either intimate or group relations. One submits to a leader, as Tocqueville put it, out of a simple desire for comfort, as a way of avoiding the pain of being independently mobile and aware. Such a withdrawal is in fact the essence of the evasion of social contact in purified communities. The feeling of being cared for under these human conditions is the joy at being taken over. Thus the structure of purification seems bound up with a feeling of human concern that is in fact a power play.

What kind of caring would exist independent of the desire for power, apart from a master and his willing slaves? This kind of caring I would call "caring about." It is closely related to a simple, creature-like curiosity, but a curiosity about graspable images, that is, individualized images. The more individual, the more particular the thing or person cared about becomes, the more men are able and willing to care about it. This kind of caring supposes that the strength of affection grows stronger the more each individual develops his or her uniqueness— there is more to care about, more to explore. The recognition that personal differences are something to love is a turning point in therapy with the marriages of schizo- phrenics. This is why the achievement of adult identity is a condition of human strength; the individual develops the power to care about individual, immediate things that may hurt him.

Socially, this kind of caring would be hostile to any abstract notion of humanity or brotherhood—hostile to any ideology, for a universalized notion of humanness is impossible for limited creatures like ourselves to grasp, and therefore to care about. This is why discussions of psychological ethics that depend on knowledge of what "the" human person is turn out to be so abstract; in the realities they care about, people do not act on the basis of a composite, fixed figure. Again, if the ideologies of the doctrinaire capitalists or of the doctrinaire Marxists seem dry and bloodless, it is perhaps because they rob men of the chance to care about something small enough to grasp, something whose dimensions are capable of being dealt with in a direct way.

This concept of care is thus a product of learning human limits, learning the limits of a person's concern and power in the world. In this way, the free curiosity of the child, the concern about immediate objects of experience in themselves, can resurface through therapy with a disturbed adult. Concern and specific care need no longer be dictated by preconceived structures of values as occurs in adolescence: things can be taken in "that don't fit" a person's sense of his identity in the world. The therapy creates a conviction of one's ability to survive, not to be annihilated by the world one doesn't yet know. This belief in the indestructibility of oneself, leading to such a capacity to care, is in its turn born of a failure to destroy the "otherness," the unknown in social experience.

Thus the complex vision of such people as a few of the young 1968 radicals comes about. Dreams of the just and perfect can remain as strong as they were in adolescence, yet there is also generated the capacity to explore and care about specific *new* things or situations not part of that ideal vision. This is the freedom of adulthood: the capacity to absorb new and perhaps painful meanings, the willingness to get involved in situations a man can't securely control. The freedom is overlaid, however, on that capacity, developed first in adolescence, to learn how to formulate lines and sequences of meaning into order to identify oneself in the social space one lives in. This juxtaposition occurs in a striking way.

Continuities Between Adulthood and
Adolescent Coherence: Chance

This double capacity, to become involved freely and yet to exercise rules for identity-making, is a complex phenomenon of psychological growth. Its significance may become clear by looking at a break made by two founders of modern psychology, William James and Sigmund Freud, from the assumptions of the Victorian era about the stages of growth to adulthood.

In child-rearing books of the middle-nineteenth century, the human being before puberty was depicted as a creature different in essence from the one that took form with the onset of sexual drives. The human being who had experienced sexual union in early adulthood was in turn conceived to be different, in emotional essence, from the adolescent. These child-books portray what can be called a *transformational* idea of human emotional development; the analogy would be that of the physical metamorphoses occurring in the growth of an insect. Both James and Freud rejected this transformational concept of development and substituted for it what could be called an *additive* idea of man's emotional development.

The nature of the human material they saw added in the course of growth was not the same, but there are some striking similarities in how they understood the process of addition to be occurring. For the new elements did not change the essence of the emotional material that came before, but rather added new, counterbalancing desires; for both James and Freud, the process of growth was thus like the continual enlargement of a mosaic. The functioning whole human being was a different man, to be sure, as he grew, but only because a new set of relationships and balances had been struck between the enlarging mosaic of emotional elements. Freud's and James's great gift to the present was to show how living creatures never shed off what they have been earlier, to show how the psychic reality of a life is not its momentary appearance but also its history.

The essence of the possible adulthood I have described is that the individual would consciously accept, and feel comfortable with, the character of growth James and Freud depict. The guilt-based need of an ill person to wipe out the past and create a totally new self, at the same time that he is a slave to the past, is absent in this state of adulthood, for concomitant with an adult's ability to let new things in for themselves, to be free, is the capacity to accept earlier states of non-freedom as part of the sum total of who he is. This acceptance of the past's mosaic makes it something the individual need not continually relive in order to change it. To bring individuals to such an acceptance is a great psychotherapeutic achievement. For, in this way, a man feels free to live in the present as a distinct, new area of experience all his own.

Both the unstable character of adulthood and the willingness of an adult to accept regressive modes of behavior in himself amount to the acceptance of *chance* in life. But to accept the chance character of emotional strength does not mean to become passive; it rather is an extension of the force of caring "about."

Such caring is not, in an adult's life, a permanent condition, nor a permanent desire, but an unstable quality that changes as the character of the individual develops and as social processes beyond the individual's control also evolve along new lines. Therapy shows that an adult man may not only feel released from being responsible for everything in his world; he may also feel that the particularities he does care about can be championed only at specific moments in time, not for always. Furthermore, he is open to losing his adulthood, through regression to modes of the past. Thus caring is a definite, natural process at a certain point—adulthood—in the life history of a man, but this full adulthood is not something permanent or ultimately triumphant: the full emotional strength of a man can be felt only as something fragile in time.

The conclusion I draw is that emotional growth is not an inevitable, one-way process, as physical growth is. This conception of adulthood as unstable helps to explain then, but not to lessen, a darker reality: the existence of so much pain in the everyday problems of ordinary life.

Because a mature creature carries all the earlier creatures he was within him, at the times when he ceases to be an adult, ceases to care about the effects of his acts, the cravings and needs of more primitive forms of life re-emerge. In terms of the pain they cause, these cravings seem to be expressions of that careless viciousness we see so often in children. It is part of their innocence to be indifferent to the effects of what they do; conversely, we think of children who do care about these effects as more "mature," no matter what their physical age.

In a sense, the identity-making powers of adolescence raise this innocent production of pain to a system. One's attention is focused on finding rules with which to create a unified self-image. The materials for these rules are not social experiences; they are rather attributes and artifacts of personality. Put concretely, an adolescent boy or girl does not think of himself as possessing a defined character by virtue of his past experience, for that experience is of a childhood inappropriate to the way he now feels; what he possesses is rather how he dresses, how he talks, the kinds of things he enjoys, his commitment to ideas. Adolescents, unlike adults, do not come to these attributes by way of sifting through experience, but by an act of conquest, of willful assimilation. And in that self-directing process lies the possibility for systematically becoming indifferent to what does not pertain to the identity one is building for oneself. The literature on normal rather than pathological adolescence offers a guide. Insensitivity in erotic and love relations can occur systematically in the search for the "ideal" lover, an ideal person who, as has been shown, is a reflection of the idealized person the young person is seeking to make of himself. Purifying identity is thus a means of making indifference a regular rule of conduct.

Regression to this systematic indifference or to the more primitive indifference of children, to their innocence in this sense, is *inevitable*. Because adult growth is additive rather than transformational, other elements of psychic reality are always present to intrude. *For this reason interpersonal pain and disorder is inevitable;* this regression forms the essence of the social reality never to be erased by any utopian arrangement of society.

The power of adolescence—and the power of even earlier stages of life to re-emerge in adulthood and so bring confusion and complexity into the lives of supposedly rational adults—affects the nature of care and concern itself.

Adulthood has been taken as a care about limited events in which the caring was not an attempt to possess or to take over. An adult caring must mean that we don't feel a possessive power over what we value; in what sense, then, can we be responsible for it?

The different chronologies of a physical and an ethical aging may clarify the problem. To possess a thing is to take it out of time, which implies that we rob it of its own destiny. To be responsible as an adult means to champion a person or thing without feeling responsible for its destiny. A concern for the here and now is precisely the sense in which good caring deals with specific and limited events in time, in a life history, and entails as well a sense of the limited vision one can have of the world in which one lives.

The center of this idea is that interpersonal pain and disorder are inevitable in *any* society. Since some societies are capable of causing more pain than others, "caring about" men and women in society must involve caring about such issues as equalizing opportunity and the sharing in the cultural and material products of the society. Utopian politics is adolescent, certainly, but no adulthood that loses such a utopian vision in the process of aging can be called a real adulthood.

Thus the comfortable reactionary adage should be reversed, to read: "Anyone can be excused for being conservative when he is eighteen, but no one can be excused for being a conservative when he is forty."

Remembrance

Adolescent strengths can also survive into adult lives through the way people define their past lives, that is, through the materials people admit into the arena of what they consciously remember.

The past life history, in terms of what adults remember, comes to be viewed through a sort of inner prism: a specific event or act, which men let into their lives and care about in and of itself, awakens a cluster of memories that is put in some order or relationship to the present. This is how traces of the need for a coherent identity remain through the connections between a panoramic past and a concrete thing cared about right now. For instance, a man may remember a painful argument with his parents; the argument may seem to embody all the arguments he ever had with them; the memory was what psychiatrists call a "crystallizing memory." Yet the power of that memory does not make him feel all arguments he has now are in the mold of that past event he recalls so well. Divorcing the panorama of his past from the new events of his present is the strength of his adulthood, just as the strength of his adolescence was learning to make the panorama. In this way an adult is free of "obsessions," of meanings and concern in the present rigidly shaped by the past life history. When therapists treat such obsessions, the object is to retain the rule-making power of an identity, but to tame it so that new matter and new meaning can permeate an individual's sense of his history.

Ethical adulthood, as caring about concrete images and events that exist on an intimate scale, would involve a capacity for remembrance of this kind. It is evident that the desire to care in this form deals with the experiences of early life as both important and yet not adequate for the present. In existential psychologies like Rollo May's this is what permits innovation in life histories. Yet for this freedom to exist, an earlier desire to give rigid shape to psycho-social realities, to remove the burdens of pain from them, *must have been acted on and the attempt failed*. In other words, for a man to have a truly malleable "historic" sense of the events in his own life, the acting out and the failure of adolescent strengths must have occurred. Otherwise, there is a compulsive need to interpret the variety of present and future experiences only in terms of the issues of the past, or worse, if the young person has never had a chance to act on the strengths emergent in his adolescence, there can remain the rest of his life the haunting sense that all the painful realities he encounters could have been avoided, if only he had once been strong enough.

This notion of remembered life history has found a great, and convoluted, expression in the work of the ego psychologist Heinz Hartmann. The sense of one's life history, Hartmann believes, must constantly shift as new events in the present transform the meaning of the past leading up to them. In the same way, each new generation of historians must reinterpret the events of a culture's past in light of the new shapes of meaning that come to fruition in the present.

What I would emphasize here is that this "historical" remembrance must emerge in adulthood from a structural failing in adolescence; the gift of this freedom comes from a social situation that permits the young to act out their painless dreams and to fail constructively.

The Social Frame

I believe the conditions of present-day society are such that this forum for acting on adolescent strengths is denied adolescents, except in the area of radical politics. If the present generation of the young seems, indeed, to be more activist, more left, than the generations before, it is perhaps a sign that they are trying to satisfy the need to act on the strengths that have emerged during their recent lives; the feeling of being threatened with a permanent adolescence has radicalized these students as much as the special social issues of the Vietnam war, poverty, and the draft.

Even today only a few young people can make a social forum out of politics for their own growth; radical politics is of necessity a limited sphere, and its guiding impulse is increasingly becoming claustrophobic and repressive. The social question for young people is still where to find an enlarged forum for experience and exploration. This, I believe, is the true task of planning modern cities. The ills of the city are not mechanical ones of better transport, better financing, and the like; they are the human ones of providing a place where men can grow into adults, and where adults can continue to engage in truly social existence.

There is a social ethic that binds the elements of this adult state together, binds the sense of limitation, the sense of caring, the hidden unities with childhood and adolescence. The desires for purification generated in adolescence are ethically a form of self-slavery, a fear of freedom. What emerges in adulthood, in chance situations and shifting grounds, is a desire for liberty, but of a special kind.

A half-century ago the German writer Max Weber sought to describe two opposing "ethics" of social involvement. These "ethics" were what Weber called an ethic of responsibility contrasted with an ethic of ultimate moral ends. A responsible act, Weber said, is always impure, always painfully mixed because of diverse motives and desires; an absolute act, on the other hand, is a struggle toward purity of desire and act, as well as toward a "pure" end. The desire for purified identity I have described clearly resembles this absolute ethic. It is a cathartic feeling for men; it leads them to dream of a world order purified of painful challenges, an order fixed, trustworthy, and predictable.

By contrast, the twisted acts Weber understood to be involved in an ethics of responsibility are close to the adult state that emerges when painless identity dreams have been tested and have failed. For an ethics of responsibility means performing acts that are impure, having a variety of motives that may even conflict with each other. And this is what accepting the mosaic of one's past will lead a man to feel about his own motives. The very diversity of these acts makes them painful: a man feels that it is impossible to set things right, to follow a simple course, to feel certain inside about what he must do. This realization replaces the self-lauding dignity of the saint or the revolutionary dreamer, the smug certitude of the respectable community leader, with the doubts of a man. What Weber sought to evoke by an ethics of responsibility was exactly that feeling of self-limitation involved in adult lives: what the self-limitation leads to, Weber said, is not a weariness and withdrawal from social situations, but a willingness to get involved in the kind of messy, disorganized social experiences that are immune to some transcendent end or justification.

Two questions are involved in such an ethics of responsibility: why are disorderly, painful events worth encountering? and why are such encounters more "responsible" than an ethics of absolute ends?

The regression from adulthood to earlier stages of life activity speaks to the first of these questions. Innate to pre-adult life, and codified in routines of adolescence, is a willful innocence of the effects of one's actions on others; that is the material from which painful dislocations and differences become innate to human society, be it socialist, capitalist, or feudal. It is the attempt of men to deal with that regression, to waken the regressor to the human "otherness" around him, that provides whatever modicum of decency and civility a society contains. This attempt to deal with "otherness," to become engaged beyond one's own defined boundaries of self, is the essence of the adulthood I envision and also the essence, I believe, of what Weber understood by an ethics of responsibility. But this means that such adult exchanges, or exchanges between someone absorbed in his own routine and someone not absorbed in it, are laden with potential for disorder and unpredictable turns. Such situations are essentially explorations, not actions out of previsualized rules. This is why disorder and painful dislocation are the central elements in civilizing social life.

It might seem, therefore, that when Weber spoke of this state of affairs as an ethics of responsibility, he meant men *ought* to experience such encounters for the sake of improving the quality of social relations. This might seem incumbent upon them, and thus a responsibility. But I believe Weber's idea had a more personal, less duty-bound meaning.

Such adult encounters mean that someone inevitably would become hurt or disoriented. But as a matter of common sense people do not *want* to be hurt or overwhelmed: men do not stare painful facts or situations in the face out of boundless desire for flagellating themselves. The point of these encounters is not that men desire to be hurt by them, but that they want something else from them, something more deeply satisfying, and they are willing to endure unforeseen consequences.

The adulthood I have described is one in which a man knows that his being cannot be annihilated by the plans of others. From failing to coherently manipulate the social space around him, the adult learns also its limits in manipulating him. John Stuart Mill expressed this as the idea that a man had no fully developed personality until he felt that his strengths, like his weaknesses, were alone and unique to him only. The act of caring about something, then, of reaching outside oneself to explore something unknown, is thus a way of reaffirming and strengthening the sense of being a full personality, by being alone at the core. The caring cannot be justified, cannot be sustaining, simply on the grounds that it is something shared between men.

Therefore this adult reaching-out is a paradox. A man becomes engaged in truly social ways, probing the "otherness" around him, in order to reaffirm the fact of his uniqueness, his adult being. The fact that a man can care about something outside himself is a sign that he has a distinctive self of his own. It is this impulse of ego affirmation, as Heinz Hartmann calls it, that creates situations of human caring.

Thus the autonomy of an adult man is not a form of isolation. Because of his knowledge that he is a real, concrete, individual being, a man is free to care about the effect of what he does in the world. Men possessed by the desire for purification do not have the power to care, as autonomous men in a world of men; they are indifferent to the effects of their acts, especially in moments of strain, because they have not developed a sense of themselves that would give them the strength to have a sense of others. Thus the American super-patriots who created the myth of "us" against "the communists" are powerless to understand the brutalizing effect of the Vietnam war on the young men they conscripted into military service. The desire for purified identity is a state of absolute bondage to the status quo; there exist few resources for analyzing how society works, only intense strengths, through the medium of coherent symbols, to transform the status quo into a generalized abstract state of life. Adult caring is more responsible, to use Weber's term, because an individual who thinks in terms of specifics is led into unknown social experience, where he makes discoveries, often terribly painful ones. That a nation like America is irresponsibly adolescent is revealed in the great fear Americans have of learning about the war they have made.

From Possible Adulthood to the "Real World"

The adult condition of life is a possibility now realized by few people. Since I have described something potential, not actual, my idea of freedom from adolescent patterns of purification may seem utopian. Yet the violence and the blind, empty coherence of present-day community life are so strong and so dangerous that a turn to looking at radical changes in the quality of social life has become a necessity. What affluent society in the last two decades has shown is that the received notions of community are in fact a way for people to hide from each other, and that the product of hiding is slavery and indifference. In place of the communal bonds men now experience, a different adult society needs to take form.

The bonds in the adult society I envision would be difficult. Care between individuals would exist only to the extent that mutual curiosity and specific personal bonds developed. There would be no expectation of human love, no community of affection, warm and comforting, laid down for the society as a whole. Human bonds would be fragmented and limited to specific, individual encounters.

Such an unstable and shifting community would have to be based on human beings who feel themselves limited, constantly changing, and unwilling to surrender their smallness to any grand vision, unwilling to make themselves whole. This would be a society involving many dissatisfactions and even much loneliness, but it would be real to the extent that men could live honestly, without myths of painless harmony.

Such a society, I believe, can arise only in the diverse disorganization of a dense city. Within adult lives, only a complex environment can give the possible complexities of men's lives full play. Since men's full ethical nature is unstable, fragile, and involved in disorganized events, only a society that is *willingly* unstable can provide, out of its own richness, a medium for growth beyond adolescence. But equally important, only a truly chaotic urban life can challenge the slavery patterns of adolescence so that large numbers of young people have the opportunity for growth now accorded only to a few. Thus can problems of therapeutic human development become the guides for understanding how cities of the future should be built.

CHAPTER SIX

The Good Uses of the City

IN THE STAGES OF ADOLESCENT GROWTH, MOST YOUNG people seem faced with an imbalance between what they are ready to experience and what they have experienced. This imbalance leads to a shortcut for experience—the creating of imaginary myths of what the world outside is like. Getting to the stages beyond this point in adolescence is now, however, very difficult for most young people. The two stages beyond are the playing out of some vision of coherent, painless life in a social environment responsive to the young person, followed by a change in concern and in the capacity for caring when the complexities of life defeat the painless myths. What happens now is that the patterns of coherence in earlier points of growth either meet no social resistance or are confined to a peculiar limbo. Where modern community life can be said to fail the young is in its inability to lead them into a social matrix where they will have to learn to deal with other people. Thus the young, whether they are radical, centrist, or conservative, can pass, and have passed, into physical adulthood with fixed pictures of themselves and a deep fear of exposing those pictures to social tests. Emotionally, then, they have failed to become adults.

What I envision is a restructuring of city life so that these adolescent patterns have a challenging social matrix. There are definite and workable means, I believe, by which cities can become human settlements that *force* these coherence drives to be tested and challenged. These same city structures could confront as well older persons who have regresssed to childish or adolescent indifference about the effect of their acts on the people around them.

Cities organized along these lines would not simply be places where the inhabitants encountered dissimilar people; the critical need is for men to have to deal with the dissimilarities. The outside world has to feel important for the dreams from within to be touched. Thus the first problem in the design of such human communities is how to plug people into each others' lives without making everyone feel the same.

Survival Communities: The Idea

The most direct way to knit people's social lives together is through necessity, by making men need to know about each other in order to survive. What should emerge in city life is the occurrence of social relations, and especially relations involving social conflict, through face-to-face encounters. For experiencing the friction of differences and conflicts makes men personally aware of the milieu around their own lives; the need is for men to recognize conflicts, not to try to purify them away in a solidarity myth, in order to survive. A social forum that encourages the move into adulthood thus first depends on making sure there is no escape from situations of confrontation and conflict. The city can provide a unique meeting ground for these encounters.

The present use of affluent community life in cities is, as shown earlier, to make it possible for men to hide together from being adults. Building a survival community where men must confront differences around them will require two changes in the structuring of city life. One will be a change in the scope of bureaucratic power in the city; the other will be a change in the concept of order in the planning of the city.

It has become standard in modern governments, though not in modern business, for bureaucracies to become pyramids of power, with the most control exercised by a few individuals at the top of the organization and increasingly less control over basic decisions exercised by the many workers below. This pyramid shape is the basis of centralized educational systems such as that of France, or legislative welfare systems like that of the United States. Businesses, on the other hand, are finding that this pyramid shape is often counterproductive. General Motors, as Peter Drucker describes it, was one of the early innovators in creating a more complex pattern of bureaucracy, and many of the businesses involved in large-scale merger or holding operations also have had to evolve similar new forms.

In the field of urban planning, the pyramid form remains endemic, despite some notable attempts to restructure it in the United States, attempts that have failed prematurely for lack of funds. Yet in order to make cities survival communities, where the affluent as well as the poor will have to deal directly with each other in order to survive, the bureacracies of control in these cities must change their form.

For certain city functions, a pyramid-shaped central organization is necessary for economies of scale. One police dispatch system is more productive than ten, one central department to control fires or to deal with sanitation better than many small ones. The problem with such central organizations is not whether they should exist, but what they should do. People today are imbued with the technological belief that the larger the structure the more inclusive should be its scope, an idea derived, again, from the nature of machine productivity; thus it is difficult to accept the idea that a strong central control apparatus can exist in the city and yet do very limited, defined tasks. Part of the difficulty in imagining this curb is that those who traditionally have wanted to limit central authority have wanted the result to be a public power vacuum, so that in the place of public power there is substituted the power of a few individuals who control the private enterprises of the city. Almost all advanced countries, with the exception of the United States, have come to understand this fallacy of "decentralization." The removal of central authority, following libertarian lines of the nineteenth century, all too often means the passing of central authority to a few private individuals who cannot be touched by the public at large.

What is needed in order to create cities where people are forced to confront each other is a reconstituting of public power, not a destruction of it. As a rule of change, the situations creating survival encounters would be as follows: there would be no policing, nor any other form of central control, of schooling, zoning, renewal, or city activities that could be performed through common community action, or, even more importantly, through direct, nonviolent conflict in the city itself. This abstract idea comes clearer by examining a second change needed in city structure.

To make the experience of conflict a maturing one requires the destruction of an assumption regnant since the work of Baron Haussmann in Paris, an assumption that the planning of cities should be directed to bring order and clarity to the city as a whole. Instead of this idea, whose basis is found in mechanical ideas of production, the city must be conceived as a social order of parts without a coherent, controllable whole form. The planning of functional divisions, of processes, of land use in advance of the habitation of the land should be abolished. Rather, the creation of city spaces should be for varied, changeable use. Areas, for example, that during one period serve as commercial places should be able in another era to serve as living places. The creation of neighborhood areas must not mean that the socioeconomic level or activities of the area are frozen by predetermined zoning specifications and the like.

This prohibition on preplanned, functional space is important because it permits great diversity to arise in city neighborhoods, and because it permits whatever social encounters and conflicts exist in the neighborhood to "take hold" in the character of the neighborhood itself. Once preplanned city space is removed, the actual use of the space becomes much more important in the lives of its users. For when predetermined use through zoning is eliminated, the character of a neighborhood will depend on the specific bonds and alliances of the people within it; its nature will be determined by social acts and the burden of those acts over time as a community's history. The preplanned "image" of city neighborhoods would not be definable on a planner's map; it would depend on how the individuals of the neighborhood dealt with each other.

Encouraging unzoned urban places, no longer centrally controlled, would thus promote visual and functional disorder in the city. My belief is that this disorder is *better* than dead, predetermined planning, which restricts effective social exploration. It is better for men to be makers of historical change than for the functional design of a pre-experiential plan to be "carried out." If the element of history in city places is allowed to re-emerge in this way, if functional dislocation and a jumble of concurrent events and peoples inhabiting common ground is permitted, then the desires for purified identity can have a testing ground of the strongest sort. This would occur in the following way.

Survival Communities: Some Examples

Let us imagine a community free to create its own patterns of life, in this case a neighborhood where cheap rents were to be found, thus likely to attract young people. Here also, if the functional divisions that now operate in city life were erased, would be found whites and blacks who were blue-collar laborers, old people living in reduced circumstances, perhaps some immigrant clusters, perhaps a few small shopkeepers. Because the land use had not been rigidly zoned, all kinds of activities appropriate to cheap rents would be found—some light manufacturing, perhaps a brothel or two, many small stores, bars, and inexpensive family restaurants.

The outstanding characteristic of this area, for the young people who move into it, would be the high level of tension and unease between the people living there. It would be a vital place, to be sure—and this is what draws urbanists like Jane Jacobs to it—but a part of the vitality would be a great deal of conflict between dissimilar groups of people. And because metropolitan-wide controls would be lessened, the threat, or the assurance, of police control would be gone, for the police would have the responsibility not of keeping peace in the community by repressing deviance but rather of dealing with organized crime or other similar problems.

Precisely because the community was on its own, because the people had to deal with each other in order to survive at all, some kind of uneasy truce between these hostile camps, these conflicting interests, would have to be arranged by the people themselves. And the act of participating in some sort of truce would force people to look at each other, if only to find areas in which some bond, tenuous and unloving as it would be, could be forged.

How would a young person feel in such a place? He would be as much a part of its life as anyone else, since controls apart from the people living there would have been lessened, especially police controls; he couldn't escape the Irish factory workers who hate the "spoiled" kids who go to college, nor the blacks who want no part of adolescent white sympathy. Yet he, and all the people around him, would have only each other; that would be the undeniable fact of life for them all. If the kids were playing records loudly, late at night, no cop would come to make them turn the record player off—the police would no longer see to that kind of thing. If a bar down the street were too noisy for the children of the neighborhood to sleep, the parents would have to squeeze the bar owner themselves, by picketing or informal pressure, for no zoning laws would apply throughout the city. Whatever happens in this city place, whatever shape the community acquires, would occur because of either the direct control or the sufferance of the people there.

Such a community would probably stimulate a young person, and yet scare him, make him want to hide, as it would everyone else, to find some nice, safe, untroubled place. But the very diversity of the neighborhood has built into it the obligation of responsibility; there would be no way to avoid self-destruction in the community other than to deal with the people who live around the place. The feeling that "I live here and I count in this community's life" would consist, not of a feeling of companionship, but of a feeling that something must be done in common to make this conflict bearable, to survive together.

Thus the impulse to hide from pain, which is at the heart of the adolescent desire for a purified identity, would have a concrete social matrix, one in which the impulse would become untenable if the person were to survive. It is hard to imagine an eighteen-year-old who suddenly has to do something to make peace with white laborers who don't like college kids and Negroes who don't like whites making a snap decision about what he will do and be in the world; he can't help seeing everything around him, he can't help having to understand differences in other people whom he may not like, and who may not like him, in order to survive. In such a complex city, a young person must become an active being, a man, and not an abstract thinker discoursing on the evils of society at large. Confronted with the need to act, to deal with human differences in order to survive, it seems plausible that the desire for a mythic solidarity would be defeated by this very necessity for survival, this need for enough knowledge of disparate people to establish a common truce.

In this way a young person could come to feel dissatisfied with his own powers for making coherent world- and self-pictures. Survival communities could give him a field, resistant to purification by him or by those around him, in which he could act on his desires for secure order and in which these desires would be defeated.

But these survival communities would lead men into adult concerns as well; they would be not merely a corrective to adolescence but a field for a richer life beyond it. The reasons for this can be understood by examining why survival communities would not escalate the expressions of social conflict into violence.

Survival Communities and Violence

Since the common pattern in the relations between men is a reversion to the willfully blind selfishness of the child, the materials for conflict are innate to social life. There are few areas in which it should be expected that men would want to work actively together. But, as in any intimate relationship, there are group relationships that can be sustaining and productive for all concerned as a result of letting conflicts of interests, emotional jealousies, class hatreds, and racial fears express themselves. These conflicts are after all as much, if not much more, a part of every human being's life as brotherly love, yet we make our children feel these are terrible, guilty secrets that should never see the light of public display. These conflicts and fears, especially now racial fears, can only be socialized if they are allowed to be expressed and play themselves out. I have never been able to understand how white liberals think they are realists when they tell their children there are no differences between blacks and

whites but cultural prejudices, as if this meant nothing in
the end. It is these cultural differences, exactly, that must
be allowed to show themselves in all their crudity and vul-
garity among both whites and blacks. Again, if the experience of meaningful conflict were possible in cities, the
young would be led to a realization of the blindness of
talking about non-negotiable demands, as the more rigid
among them do now. It is in the essence of experiences of
conflict, when the conflict matters for survival, that men
learn to talk to their enemies, learn to see the dimensions
of that which they oppose.

It is one of the terrible simplicities of modern city life
that we believe the expression of these hostile feelings
will lead to violence. Perhaps the reason this belief is so
widely held is that it justifies repression of our feelings,
and so lets us hide from them, as we assume that once
they are out in the open, only chaos can be the result.
This is similar to that adolescent metaphor by which guilt
over a specific transgression is transformed into a much
broader self-definition—that "I am a sinner"—so that the
act or feeling itself can be denied as a reality to be dealt
with.

Yet if men do not grow out of this denial, if men continue to believe that hostility between groups should be
muted, not encouraged in its social expression, the cities
will continue to burn, for nothing exists socially now to
mediate hostility, to force people to look beyond their
images of threatening outsiders to the actual outsiders
themselves. By restructuring the power of city bureaucracies so that they leave to the hostile groups themselves

the *need* to create some truce, in order for chaos to be prevented, hostility can take on more open and less violent forms.

Certainly, this is to gamble with social life itself. Yet it is of the essence of adult lives that chance and chance situations should provide the medium for new insight and a new understanding of discrete, other beings. To assure tranquillity in advance is to revert to a dream of painless immunity, and ultimately, if we are to judge from some social revolutions of our own time, to bring on a totalitarian rigidity for the sake of the dream.

Releasing conflict between groups in survival communities is not as great a gamble as it might seem. Certain processes, connected with the final stage of transition from adolescence to adulthood, ensure at least some measure of social peace, I believe, because of changes wrought in the individual involved in the web of social conflict between diverse urban groups.

Survival Communities and Adulthood

In any large central city, there remain today many differences in life styles that could be used to distribute conflict, or at least fragment it. Ethnicity, social class, and race are not simple conditions of life, but complex factors that tend to interpenetrate and become diffused. For instance, it is a popular error to suppose that the violence of recent summers in American cities is a "race" phenomenon, for most middle-class blacks are not only uninvolved but also hostile to the Negro militants; however, given the structure of community life and police control in American cities, middle-class blacks and poor blacks never have to deal with each other about their common ties or differences; each can sink back into a comfortable disgust over what the other group does. Yet if they had to confront each other, if the police stopped their blanket repression and gave the segments of the black community the responsibility to control themselves, these hostilities could be expressed, and both groups, in order to survive, would find that they could go no further to achieve their own ends without finding out something about each other. Let us imagine added to this situation a refusal of the police to intervene between any black group and the whites who now feel threatened by them. I believe that, instead of massive violence erupting, the people involved would learn that there is too much complex feeling involved to be taken care of by the burning of stores. When people have to come face to face in order to survive, the death instinct does not prevail; it is only when men are alienated from using their own power, from being real men, that they burn themselves out and invite massive repression from the outside.

In other words, if we could increase the complexity of confrontation and conflict in the city, not polarize it, the aggression, still there, would channel itself into paths that allow at least mutual survival. This, I believe, is not as grim a prospect as it might seem. For when a man fails to achieve coherent ends, when there is too much complexity impinging on him for him to advocate something "pure and simple," the failure that results leads not to dissolution of his social resolve, but to exactly that state of mind now open only to a few among those who have experienced revolutionary conflict. As a consequence of this failure, one wants to understand the complexity that defeated one; the sense of curiosity can be awakened, has to be awakened, if a man is going to know enough in order to survive.

This is how the adult's kind of care, independent of some painless order in which he is safe, comes into being. It is a caring based on the curiosity and commitment to the immediate, impinging social world rather than an otherworldly love or an urge toward purity. The French psychologist Georges Lapassade has said that adulthood is a stage in which pleasure and pain are no longer separable, because the individual is engaged by choice in situations without an end, situations that are "unachieved." It is exactly the character of these survival communities to create "unachieved" situations that have no clear form or definition in advance of the experience of social interaction. By willfully making the question of social survival depend on the confused impure actions men take, these adult capacities to care and to wonder about the unknown will be generated. By a fundamental paradox of psychosocial development, the primitive questions of intergroup survival must resurface for a more civilized and mature life to exist.

The question may be posed as to what is particularly "urban" about such communities of survival. What role does the city as a special human settlement play in this communal movement to adulthood?

Survival Communities as Cities

The structural conditions under which survival communities could work are, first, those of heavy population density and, second, those of multiple contact points. Both of these structures are brought to a high point in urban settlements.

The first of these conditions seems readily apparent. If people are to deal with an environment too complex to control, a small village or a suburb, with its intimacy and isolation, will hardly suffice. There needs to be an enormous number of people packed together for a truly uncontrollable environment to exist. But what if this mass simply acted as a little group enlarged? It is here that the real promise of city life begins, for as the number of people concentrated together in one place grows very large, the quality of human relations changes.

This appears more obvious than it is. In fact, those writers of the past two decades who have confused a "mass-culture" society with an increasingly urban one have ignored the fact that cities of the postwar era have become less dense and their population dispersed over a wide area even as the numbers in the megalopolis, as Jean Gottman calls it, have increased. There are definite reasons why a massive, dense city society is opposed to a mass-culture society.

The first of these is the possibility, indeed the encouragement, of deviance in urban places. The first great American urban sociologist, Robert Park, wrote of the

dense cities of his time that exactly because so many people were packed together it was hard for central agencies
of control like the police to see all those who were different, or to control them through coercive means. Numbers provided, he said, a kind of screen for deviations or
idiosyncrasies; a man will not be noticed or forced into
a community-wide mold with anything like the pressure
found in a small town or suburb. Researches since Park's
time bear this idea out in many ways. It is known that
sexual deviations are much more easily expressed in
dense urban areas than in the careful watching of the
suburb or small town. Historically, deviant subcultures,
be they bohemian, ethnic, or, today, youth and student,
survive much longer in dense urban areas than in sparsely
populated, easily controlled areas.

The second reason large dense communities are freed
from the controls inherent in small ones concerns the instability of their populations. Jane Jacobs and other popular writers are greatly at fault for looking at the dense
ethnic inner-city areas as traditionally stable places where
people got to know their neighbors through years and
years of common association. Historically and demograph-
ically this has not been true. There has been and is a great
deal of movement from place to place within dense cities
and between them. The warm associations Jacobs found
are due to factors other than population stability. (I do
not wish to quarrel with the ethical values she sees in
dense city places; she simply ascribes them to the wrong
factual base.)

The effect of this population movement in cities, so
much greater than the intra-communal movement found

in suburbs, is to destroy the power of tight-knit structures or local rules on the citizenry. The popular stereotype of Italian or Jewish urban communities as closed and impenetrable is flawed, because the people in them are continually moving around. That kind of tightness more likely occurs in the white, middle-class suburb, for the rate of household movement is lesser there when compared to the second generation in any of the inner-city groups.

Large numbers of people living densely packed together thus provides the medium of diversity and instability necessary for these survival communities to operate. But one may object that this instability makes it impossible for people to be able to face each other, to become involved with those around them. It *is* impossible as long as we understand coming together in community action along the old lines of common endeavor and a sharing of similarity. But the kinds of contacts that once existed in these ethnic ghettos suggest how direct, face-to-face associations might actually be encouraged under conditions of instability and diversity.

In the old ghetto order, multiple contact points with diverse people and groups in the city were necessary, since none of the institutions in that era of scarcity had the power to be self-sustaining. By removing centralized bureaucracies of social control and by eliminating preplanning with restrictive zoning, the same effect could be reproduced today; the intimate institutions of city life would not be able to be self-sustaining, and the individual or family would have to look beyond their own borders in order to survive. Decentralization, as the idea is used here, would have the effect of necessitating multiple social contacts for survival, without leading to community cohesion.

This process can be illustrated as follows. Let us suppose that a city university were deprived of its special zoning and centralized controls. Like Columbia, Harvard, or the University of Chicago, its students and faculty would live in a heterogeneous area with many hostile non-university people intermixed among the school population. But unlike these three schools, the city university we envision would not possess the power of eminent domain, nor police protection for students as well as faculty, and would be forbidden to use its money for coherent territorial acquisition. I believe such an arrangement would force a communal confrontation of the diverse elements that necessitate exploration of the "otherness" of all sides. An attempt would have to be made to survive together in the midst of great tension through finding out something about each other. In this way people would begin to think beyond the convenient fictions of the "administration," the "student movement," or the "community." When men and women must deal with each other as people, in a community where there is no overriding control to ensure survival, the flight into abstraction becomes unreal. The complexities of conducting a community life together are going to make the generalized pictures *disfunctional*, because concrete men and women simply will not act in the predictable ways generalized pictures would indicate. Acting on the level of mythic "we" and "they," there is no contact between the concrete beings who must work out some arrangements in order to survive each day. If power were decentralized in this way, a multiple chain of contacts, between people living in the same block, or working in the same area, would be necessary. Since the people would be diverse, the web of affiliation for sheer survival would become particularized, not abstracted into "us" against the outside.

In fact, just such a mutual adjustment process occurred in New York's much maligned school district I.S. 201. During the few weeks that this project had to operate on its own, conditions *within* the affected schools were remarkably nonviolent between Jewish white teachers, black teachers, and their black, Puerto Rican, and poor white students. Paths of real accommodation were beginning to emerge. Once the strike forced a we-they confrontation with a central authority—the teacher's union—the level of violence and the easy images of "us and them" behind violent encounters again became dominant.

Multiple contacts necessitated by dense, decentralized social conditions, such as those occurring within this school district, illustrate a process well thought out in Lewis Coser's *The Functions of Social Conflict*. This is the binding power of face-to-face tension and conflict, as opposed to the destructive power of conflict between bureaucratic institutions. For the experience of expressing hostility or simply an alternative to the acts or the feelings of someone else creates a certain kind of mutual commitment. People are dealing with each other, willing to express themselves, rather than storing up their grievances in private, where the character of their enemies and themselves becomes black-and-white clear. Multiple points of contact with different elements in a city diffuse hostility to the point where an individual will despair of defining some safe, secure attributes of his own identity and social space. This sense of failure is precisely the point at which he begins to become an adult and to feel that his identity instead turns on his very power to reach out and explore.

In these dense, diverse communities, the process of making multiple contacts for survival would burst the boundaries of thinking couched in homogeneous small-group terms. Since urban space would not be preplanned into separate units, as it now is, but would be free for all manner of incursions and combinations, the neat categories of spatial experience in cities, such as home, school, work, shopping, parks, and playgrounds, could not be maintained. They would come to interpenetrate, as Jane Jacobs observed in the dense inner-city community of New York where she lived, or as Robert Park once observed in Chicago. However, now such interpenetration would not just be part of the local color of the ethnic working class but a part of the life of more affluent people as well. Men would find in the places where they worked community problems and community experiences, as well as community conflicts, not limited to the sphere of their own small jobs, just as the region where a man lived would not be immune to a diverse circle of influences and modes of life. If an increased density in the planning of cities was connected to a limiting of central bureaucratic authority, spheres of multiple contact like this in the opportunities for city-wide action would emerge, as would the necessity to act in a direct and personal way.

The kind of urban community life I have in mind has specific as well as general guidelines. What I should like to explore now is the techniques by which this kind of community life might actually be realized in the future planning of cities.

Some Suggestions for Action

It might seem that the tone of this essay would preclude a discussion of planning: isn't an uncontrolled environment innately an unplanned one? Yet I disagree with some community thinkers who believe that diverse communities can arise naturally and spontaneously, once "the system" is destroyed. I believe diverse communities do not arise spontaneously, nor are spontaneously maintained, but instead have to be created and urged into being. Let me try to show from the critical perspectives of this book why this is so.

The suburbanization and increasing organization of city spaces into functional compartments is not a process arbitrarily imposed on city people but one responsive to their human desires, the desires to hide from pain and disorder. The idea that the "people" are straining at the bit against the "system" is much too naïve, requires that all these dark elements of fear and cowardice in the process of growing be denied. More realistically, the people and the system are in conspiracy with each other to establish a comfortable slavery to the known and the routine.

Furthermore, the social dimensions of affluence in city life show themselves easily put to the service of such voluntary slavery. For affluence weakens the need for sharing of scarce goods and services, and lends each man the power to buy or control the survival necessities for his everyday activities.

Given this disposition, both in the development of men and in the immediate past history of city communities, there seems to be little reason to think that creating a power vacuum, by simply abolishing the present "system," is going to lead to a millennial flowering. People have an innate impulse to recapitulate under different names the slaveries they have known in the past. This is what revolutionary thinkers like Fanon have understood so well, and what the "community revolutionaries" have yet to learn. Some positive directions toward change are necessary.

The first of these directions is to increase the visible density of urban areas. Unfortunately, high-density living space is now planned only along the lines of a suburban model. The large housing projects, like Lefrak City in New York, have all their functions neatly prelabeled and separated, so that although many people live together they seldom come into unknown, unplanned contact. If these parts were jumbled together, the density of these housing projects would serve a social purpose. This can be done in a number of ways.

High-rise buildings should be thought of, Frank Lloyd Wright once said, as vertical streets. Instead of putting all the common meeting places on the ground or on the top stories, the public places should be distributed throughout the buildings. Wright's "Mile-High City" contained some of these ideas in embryo.

But a more direct and perhaps more practical way of establishing visible density in cities has already been developed historically. In the great squares of such cities as Paris or Florence, unlike those of London, the arrangement of townhouses around a common space provided a superb mingling ground for the residents. The density of these areas, as portrayed in Arnold Zucker's *Town and Square* was very high, even in modern terms. We do know, for example, that townhouse blocks with spacious quarters have been designed to provide a density almost approaching that of the high-rise towers which are isolated on their plots of land, the open space walled by chain-link fencing. In contrast, the square surrounded by townhouses makes human density count socially. Such density permits the expression of personal deviation or idiosyncrasy in a milieu where there are too many people thrown together to discipline everyone to the same norm. The visible density of such places, if past patterns are a guide, increases the mobility and flow of the population.

This mixing together of dense numbers of people requires in its turn a second direction of change: a concerted effort to effect socioeconomic integration of living, working, and recreational spaces. In the United States, this would extend to trying to push integration racially. Since this idea is anathema to sectors of both the Left and the Right, I should spell out first how it is practicable, and second why it is absolutely necessary to restore a truly civilized city life.

In the rebuilding of Paris by Baron Haussmann, socioeconomic integration of housing units was in some cases attempted. The new apartment units contained the rich, the middle class, and the poor. As David Pinckney points out in his book on the subject, the rich occupied the lower floors, the middle classes the middle floors, and the poor the roof garrets. The system worked for a long time, and contributed, Pinckney points, to the sense of diversity and vitality in central-city Paris. Since Haussmann's time, only sporadic and halfhearted efforts have been made to continue this form of residential building. In the United States, there have been a few such attempts within government housing, but the mixing of rich and middle class or middle class and poor has always been radically weighted at one end or the other, and the actual apartment groups kept separate socioeconomically. Real estate interests have said over and again that in private apartments or housing developments this homogeneity is a necessity imposed on the builder, because people feel uncomfortable unless they know that their neighbors are mostly like themselves.

True enough, but the point is that it would be *better* in the end if they did feel uncomfortable, and began to experience a sense of dislocation in their lives. If it takes government money to assist in this socioeconomic mixing, then the money ought to be spent. Again, the spontaneous character of people's desires is no guide to social virtue. The government has subsidized some integration, but hardly enough, and hardly in the kind of living space where people would have to come to terms with each other's presence.

Certain U.S. planners have objected that this mixing of classes, which would result in the mixing of races as well, has brought only unbearable racial conflict, and is inhumane to enforce when both sides don't want it. The public housing projects these people point to certainly have been miserable failures. But this is a very biased picture. The sociologist Thomas Pettigrew has estimated that there are a large number of communities in the United States outside the South that are integrated house by house rather than with a Negro "sector," and that at least passable relations have been achieved. There are also, despite the current stereotype of anti-black feeling among white workers, a large number of inner-city communities that are racially integrated areas containing white working class and black working class. The levels of violence, as measured by the incidence of high school violence and the like, is *lower* in these communities than in either homogeneously white or black working-class neighborhoods. There is tension to be sure, but it isn't escalated to violence. The difficulty is that as long as people keep thinking of the majority of blacks as unemployed misfits and the white working class as authoritarian haters, this comfortable sense of the impossibility of racial integration can be maintained.

A more serious challenge to the practicality of racial integration in cities is that offered by such writers as Norman Podhoretz. In his essay "My Negro Problem, and Ours" Podhoretz describes the strong anti-Negro feeling of Jews, and the anti-Semitic feeling of blacks, in an integrated situation where both groups are enmeshed in poverty. It may be that, for blacks and whites in poverty, socioeconomic integration of housing and schools would be only an inhuman and brutalizing experience, being thrust among those who have made it or are about to rise. However, all the popular stereotypes treating "the urban problem" as essentially one of poverty ignore the fact that the majority of urban blacks are not destitute but are working class and lower middle class. They, like their white working-class compeers, have been dealt out of the *qualitative* opportunities wealthier people in the city can have. Once one gets above the poverty line, racial integration is practicable, and has, in the cases where it has been permitted to take hold, proved to be a viable community structure. It is also, I would argue, qualitatively necessary, for the same reasons that socioeconomic integration is.

It is the mixing of such diverse elements that provides the materials for the "otherness" of visibly different life styles in a city; these materials of otherness are exactly what men need to learn about in order to become adults. Unfortunately, now these diverse city groups are each drawn into themselves, nursing their anger against the others without forums of expression. By bringing them together, we will increase the conflicts expressed and decrease the possibility of an eventual explosion of violence.

It has been said over and over by black community organizers that integration attempts only fragment further the sense of selfhood and self-dignity of ghetto residents. This may be true below the lines of poverty. But for the large segment of the urban black population that has become or is becoming middle class, I am convinced that this cultural insularity will lead in the end to the same kind of dullness and routine experienced by white ethnic groups that have become both prosperous and self-enclosed. Class and wealth *do* make a difference in people's lives. What we need to find are community forms that are affirmative and growth-producing for men freed from the boundaries of poverty, and such communities seem to me possible only when diverse and ineradicably different kinds of people are thrown together and forced to deal with each other for mutual survival.

It may be that ethnic and racial differences would eventually be weakened in such communities. The point is that concord would not therefore be reached; the inevitable disruptions caused by regression to childhood selfishness would still be present. But in dense, visibly diverse communities where people would have to deal with each other, these regressions would provide a constant starting point for conflict and conciliation. The racial, ethnic, and economic shadings that now exist in city life are places to begin in forming communities where this confrontation occurs.

Diversifying the community through such integration raises the third, and most important, direction of replanning cities for such adult growth: the removal of central bureaucracies from their present directive power.

The closest that community workers in the last decades came to a theory of community control was the belief that functions carried on in city hall ought to be "decentralized," turned over to local community groups. When this kind of decentralization has been practiced, which is rarely, and is limited to the black ghetto, it has produced some results. Hostile white school or government administrators have been replaced by less hostile black administrators. In a very few cases, the change actually meant the man on the street could begin to grapple with the environment around him and worry about changing it. But the problem with this view of decentralization, especially where it applies to the broader, nonpoverty society outside the ghetto, is that no changes of power *in essence* are involved. In other words, localism doesn't bring a change in the seat of power, so that the individual has to act for himself. Suburbs, after all, are decentralized, local units of power, and yet the only community-control exercises at this level which grip the inhabitants are acts of repressing deviates: i.e., fights about open housing, gerrymandering of school districts, and the like.

Really "decentralized" power, so that the individual has to deal with those around him, in a milieu of diversity, involves a change in the essence of communal control, that is, in the refusal to regulate conflict. For example, police control of much civil disorder ought to be sharply curbed; the responsibility for making peace in neighborhood affairs ought to fall to the people involved. Because men are now so innocent and unskilled in the expression of conflict, they can only view these disorders as spiraling into violence. Until they learn through experience that the handling of conflict is something they have to deal with, something that cannot be passed on to police, this polarization and escalation of conflict into violence will be the only end they can frame for themselves. This is as true of those who expect police reprisals against themselves, like the small group of militant students, as those who call in the police "on their side."

In a less extreme dimension, the spending of money for neighborhood schools or civic improvements is meaningless when the neighborhood school or committee is merely spending money along lines sent down from a central authority. How and why the money is to be spent needs to be the responsibility of the people who will feel its impact. In the first case, central authority is retained under the guise of "decentralization"; in the second case the nature of the power truly changes.

We also need to explore how a centralized state apparatus can be made compatible with decentralized ends. There is no reason why centralized resources, like taxes, fire and police services, health and welfare benefits, have to be destroyed in order to decentralize power in essence. The community leaders who advocate this make a mistake: it is not the existence of centralized structures which is *per se* the evil, but the machinelike uses to which these structures are so easily directed. Conceivably through social experiment we can learn how to distribute centralized resources to create decentralized, uncontrolled social situations. The essence of bureaucracies, Simmel wrote, is the use to which they are put; these impersonal structures are corrupting only when they are taken as ends in themselves, when the processes by which they work most efficiently are taken to be an image of how society itself ought to function. By breaking this machine image, and removing from massive bureaucracies the power to regulate conflict, we may be able to invent new activities for them in which they help create diversity and disorder rather than stifle it.

These suggestions for a greater density, diversity, and power relations in city communities would create in general a high level of tension. They would not create a stifling sense of localism, of "urban villages" in Herbert Gans's term; instead, they would create a sense of the need to deal with shifting combinations of people and shifting issues over the course of time in order to keep daily life ongoing. I don't imagine any sort of joyous communion in these encounters but rather a feeling of needing to keep in touch, a feeling of having to be involved in a social world.

A disordered, unstable, direct social life of this kind would lead to structural changes in the city itself as well as to the individuals in the social milieu.

New City Institutions

Cities made disorderly along these lines produce at least three kinds of institutional change. First, there would be a radical broadening of people active as the city's planners and leaders. Second, political "image" or personality would become a less important factor in choosing elected officials. Third, and most importantly, the phenomenon of family intensity would be greatly weakened.

The first two of these changes are fairly apparent. The "experts" on planning would become people who know something about the problems besetting peculiar places in the city at given moments in time, rather than men drawing maps of the new metropolitan "whole" in a central office. The experts would qualify by virtue of their experience in a community and their capacity to act effectively in its terms. This doesn't mean, as was so naïvely thought in many of the community development programs of the

1960's, that a man is an expert on a particular place simply because he lives there. It does mean that the old professional boundaries are broken down, and people with particular talents for dealing with special situations, talents developed out of experience as well as out of prior training, can put them to use. The filtering out of these effective people now occurs because the aims of planning are for an abstract whole supposedly encompassing all the particularities. For example, a real estate man who knows a lot about the conditions in a small sector of a large city, but is no expert on the whole city, is much less likely to be consulted by city hall than an executive in a large firm who thinks in the urban-wide, abstract terms of property-balancing, metropolitan-wide growth, and the like. The latter has much more economic power, to be sure, but his social effectiveness and usefulness can actually be much less than the smaller man who deals in specific community terms.

In other words, the feeling of being socially important in the life of a city spreads to the degree that unity in the planning of cities is weakened. More people are engaged, but they will produce conflicting results that will not add up to a satisfying picture of the urban whole.

The political results will be uncomfortable for those imbued with the notion of "progressive" urban reform. The product of such decentralization will be political machines; this was the case when urban power was badly fragmented at the turn of the century, and I believe it will become the case again. Yet there is no need to recapitulate the personal graft involved in that era. What will emerge is an evaluation of political leaders in terms of how much they can respond to and "deliver" to diverse communities and groups. Moynihan has wisely observed that charismatic "image" leaders appeal to people who are relatively passive in city affairs. When people become active, they begin evaluating political power in terms of effective networks, because they have defined for themselves their needs or their desires in terms of action. Most of the old machine politicians were distinctly lacking in beautiful clothes and clean-cut expressions, but they were responsive to concrete problems put in this way.

The idea is repellent, perhaps, because of the kinds of machine-politician leaders at work today. But they have oppressive power precisely because they have captured the centralized bureaucracies for their own ends. By fragmenting the power of these bureaucracies, politicians of the stripe of the present mayor of Chicago would be forced back into a more modest, less dictational mold: uncharismatic, sensing that their power lies in how well they distribute the goods of the state. City politicians would become "middlemen" rather than beautiful leaders; they would be successful to the extent that they channel the revenues and coercive power of the state down to the level where it could be used as materials for communities engaged in formulating the rules of their own survival.

This may seem utopian, but it is much less dangerous than the utopia invoked now every election day, when one is told to vote for the cleansing savior, the charismatic leader who will restore order and decency. Decentralization is dismissed as visionary by the very people who vote, not out of interest or conviction, but out of longing for the pure leader who will "save" them and the city, state, or country.

The family would be the most deeply affected by cities reorganized along these lines. Dense, disorderly cities would challenge the capacity of family groups to act as intensive shelters, as shields from diversity. For the whole thrust of these urban places will be to create a feeling of need in the individual that he has to get involved in situations outside the little routines of his daily life in order to survive with the people around him. The illusion that the family is a predictable microcosm of the larger society will be difficult to maintain under such conditions, for new problems will always be entering the circle of a man's survival concerns. The illusion that all family members are equals in experiential understanding will be equally difficult to support. In such an environment, it will be obvious to the adults not only that *they* are being pulled into different experiences from their children, but also that the children will inevitably be moving in different circles of experience from them. Generational tensions are, to be sure, unbridgeable events in the life cycle, but the degree of pain and feeling of desertion they entail depends on the social milieu as much as on the individuals involved. In a society where men could actually experience constant social change in their own lives, the inevitable dislocations involved in the change of generations could be borne with more grace.

The more the primacy of the family is challenged by multiple points of social contact, the stronger the family will become. This strength will occur not as a resistance to the outside but as the very result of being limited by a complex outer world. Affluent urban families, as I have tried to show, experience peculiar dislocations because they are burdened with too much. These families are twisted because men look to them for rules about a great diversity of social activities, activities that do not naturally take place within the home. Were these excess pressures removed, by the *necessity* for looking elsewhere to assure the ongoing survival of one's social life, the family group would become a more satisfying arena of its own. For example, marriages now occur for the majority of urban affluent couples in the United States on or before the age of legal adulthood. It is only a minority who give themselves a breathing space between emergence from their past family lives into new family responsibilities. Were cities constructed so that the young person was being pulled in a number of directions as he emerged into adulthood, drawn into different areas of interest and concern, perhaps the desire to wait a while before settling down would be kindled. In other words, people might begin to learn to wait until they were formed adults, with some free experience of their own, before committing themselves to another person. Alfred Adler once expressed this as learning to be alone in order to have the strength to be together. Learning to be alone does not occur in isolation; an environment like the dense disorderly city could promote it and make it feel a positive achievement.

By providing a wide network of social contact that the people of a city must use in order to survive, the polarization of intimacy in the home circle and the impersonal functional tasks in the world beyond might be erased. The conflicts of this city society would provide a web of confrontations whose character and personnel, unlike the family group, would be constantly in flux. This sounds as though anarchy is being brought into the city as a positive principle; that is exactly what I intend, but anarchy of a form not envisioned by the anarchist writers of the past.

CHAPTER SEVEN

---

*The City as
an Anarchic System*

TOWARD THE END OF THE NINETEENTH CENTURY A SMALL band of men instituted a wave of assassinations, bombings, and other terrorist acts in the name of what they called anarchism. As a consequence anarchism in many countries became a proscribed doctrine, and anarchists criminals in the eyes of the law. Anarchism literally means "without government" or "without control" (an-archy). The term became overlaid with violent and terrorist associations in the late nineteenth century for peculiar reasons.

E. H. Carr has said that anarchism in the last century was a critique of society, not a plan for social reconstruction. The virtues of being without government were conceived as correctives to the emerging industrial order, and it was difficult for anarchists to think about an anarchic society as having an ongoing life of its own. Therefore, although the rigidities and injustice of the industrial order gave the anarchists a powerful rationale for what they were against, the terms of their own thinking never told them what they were really fighting for. The Marxian terms, on the other hand, did.

Originally, anarchists and Marxians were part of the same fledgling movement. Proudhon, taken by many to be the first anarchist, thought of himself as a disciple of socialism; his ideas for "federalism" in the conduct of just social affairs were hardly plans for life without government. But as the anarchist idea ripened, as the fact of disorder seemed to become in itself a challenge to the manufacturers, anarchists moved away from the discipline and the search for internal structure that characterized the First International of the Marxian socialists. It was the Russian Bakunin who personified this movement away from organized socialism; he was an intense, childlike rebel who made his sense of outrage at the cruelties around him a self-sufficing state of mind rather than a springboard for trying to change society.

I believe this limitation of the anarchists' vision, this static quality of their rejection, is what led them to violence and terrorism at the century's end. For, lacking a notion of what should be instituted when injustice was overthrown, these men were naturally drawn to look at the act of rejection as a moral region of its own. The more powerful the process of rejecting, the more complete, the more purging an event it would be. If, unlike the Marxians, all they had was the fact of saying no, their statement had to be cataclysmic, had to be everything. This was the path by which Georges Sorel, the great anarchistsyndicalist writer, was led to see violence as a great purging, cleansing act in society. The violent catharsis was so great that what happened after seemed petty and anti-climactic.

The ideas about anarchy in cities advanced so far in this essay are inherently hostile to the enshrinement of violence to which the anarchist movement of the nineteenth century was finally led. For I have tried to look at what society should be like once it is freed of economic injustice and becomes affluent. Now, I believe, disorder is an enduring way to use the wealth and abundance of modern times; the result of this anarchy in abundant city life will be to decrease the need for violence rather than idealize the desire for it.

Such statements as there are on post-revolutionary social structure by nineteenth-century anarchists lean to a society antithetical to the dense, diverse city. Among the greatest virtues of the Paris commune, to men like Proudhon, was its small-group character and tightness. Carr has pointed to the same desire for little, intimate communities in Bakunin's beliefs and in those of his fellow countryman Kropotkin, who looked back to the village community of the late medieval period. After the purging cataclysm of violent overthrow, the tight little band of believers—this is today Fanon's dream as well. It is a millennial vision bound to decay, for such little communities permit the flourishing of desires for solidarity, and these desires in turn repress creative, disruptive innovations in life style and belief.

Unlike the anarchists of his time, Marx envisioned the shape of post-revolutionary society, and discussed mechanisms that would make disorder, constant change, and expanding diversity its hallmarks. But he assumed these things would come to pass of themselves, once economic injustices were routed. Marx refused to explore the possibility that rigid order, a fear of change, and a desire for sameness were innate to human beings, were generated by the very processes of human maturation. Seen in a different light, his refusal was an article of belief in the basic dignity of men. His hopes for a natural liberation, in light of the psychological researches that followed him and the experiences of "liberated nations" who have become affluent, seem now no longer possible to entertain. In an affluent world, be it pre- or post-revolutionary, the real problem is for men to be encouraged to abandon their deep-down natural desire for a comfortable slavery to the routine. This encouragement is what purposely dense, purposely decentralized, purposely disordered cities could provide.

But the question arises as to how such cities could endure as social systems. Isn't it a contradiction in terms to talk of an anarchic environment as enduring, and therefore somehow stable? Furthermore, wouldn't men, faced with the disorder, gradually give it up and return to the more comfortable slaveries of the past?

Some Social Possibilities of Affluence

The modern social use of technology has been to provide men with a coherent image of order—order consisting of actions that are performed by passive agents. A machine in which one part or operation deviates from its preconceived use makes the whole go out of order, and stop functioning. The usual modes of urban planning are executed in such metropolitan, "system" terms, derived from the model of machine productivity.

This image of technology ignores its true and humane social use, a use that makes practicable the system of social disorganization men need in order to become adults. For the productive capacities of modern industry, technologically in excess of what is needed for a society's bare survival, permit a greater range and complexity of conflict than under scarcity conditions. Labor union strikes are a good example of this. In prosperous sectors of the economy where strike funds and personal income are developed, the occurrence of a strike does not mean that the conflict becomes a question of whether the workers are brought to the starving point or the company to bankruptcy; the affluence provides a certain floor to the conflict. The material base of the economy is such that social conflicts need not escalate to life or death struggles between the parties involved.

Sociologists have usually looked at such a flooring to the economic disaster caused by group conflict as a sign of the emergence of social solidarity and sameness in a culture. Supposedly, the less cataclysmic a conflict, the less the desire or need for it. This entirely misses the point. This economic floor, which is the result of technological affluence, can actually permit *greater* regions of conflict than in scarcity societies, because the stakes of group conflict need not escalate to the point where one of the parties must obliterate the other.

One of the most ridiculed and most feared innovations of American social planning in the last decade was the federal government's establishment of funds for local groups to use in pressing their demands against city hall and state agencies. This program could have had an enormously creative impact had it been adequately funded, for the government revenues were used by decentralized groups to fight only for the programs they wanted. With such a flooring they did not have to fight city hall for their economic existence as well; the existence of the groups were not dependent on the success or failure they had in funding particular programs. The local organizations did not need to tie themselves to a fixed ideology or function in order to stay alive, but were permitted an independent existence. Thus they were free to grow and change direction. The point about an affluent society is that there is enough money around for this kind of economic "flooring" of conflict groups to be created. The amounts of money needed are not really large compared to the massive outlays made for nonproductive military activities. When such "flooring" exists, so that conflict over particular issues need not escalate to the level of whether one or the other of the parties must be destroyed, the organizations can attain a great deal more internal flexibility in their goals and programs.

The proper uses of technological abundance, then, permit a social conception of survival *different* from that obtaining in the scarcity economies of the past. Survival comes to be defined in terms of concrete actions taken to change behavior of individuals or groups in opposition: the slavery of a material reference point of existence, as Marx called it, does not interfere with this experiential interaction. In this way, Marx's idea of a post-revolutionary anarchy would touch on the city anarchy envisioned here.

Putting abundance to such social ends, as has occurred in both American and European labor unions and intermittently for local community organizations, is one way that disordered relationships and conflict grouping could practicably have an ongoing life. Unlike the conflicts in times of scarcity, survival is framed in terms of whether people will be able to communicate with each other, not whether they will be able to stay alive. Again I am forced to refer to Marx: he believed that in an abundant society permanent disorder is possible because survival depends on social acts and experiences rather than the brute possession of material goods.

But there is another reason why the disordered city can have an ongoing, viable existence, a reason not referable to such theories as those of Marx.

Stability Through Direct Aggression

Aggressive feelings are inherent in people's lives, but aggression itself is a little-understood phenomenon. Psychologists and anthropologists have bitterly debated the question of why aggression exists to a much greater degree in men than in other animals. Some researchers claim aggression is the result of frustration and therefore developed in the course of a life in individual ways and through personal experiences; others claim aggression to be an instinctual response, existing in the psychic make-up of men in advance of any of their particular experiences. Whatever the origin of aggression, the fact of its importance in men's social activities cannot be denied.

The structures modern affluent communities are built on are such that basic aggression is denied outlets other than violence. Because the images of social order are functional images of preset roles to be played so that the social whole will function, aggressive behavior among the players seems at best to be a diversion from the proper workings of the community, and at worst a threat to the very idea of achievement and accomplishment. "Aggression resolution" is regarded as necessary for further group action to occur.

But if aggression is so deeply engraved in the life of men, then a society that regards aggressive outbreaks as a hindrance rather than as a serious human experience is hiding from itself. Indeed, one school of social thought now considers modern ideas for sublimating aggression, such as directing attacks away from their original targets into more socially manageable forms, as actually conducive to the kind of emotional buildup that can suddenly burst forth in acts of unprovoked violence.

The clearest example of the way this violence occurs is found in the pressures on police in modern cities. Police are expected to be bureaucrats of hostility resolution, unresponsive to taunts and attacks on them, passive in the performance of enforcing set rules on an unruly or violent clientele. Apart from all the theories about ethnic hatreds, "working-class authoritarianism," and the like now invoked to explain police riots, is it any wonder, in simple human terms, that the imperative to respond passively has a terrible effect on these men? The need to work aggression out of their systems builds up to the point where they have to brutalize indiscriminately when unleashed on their own. A society that visualizes the lawful response to disorder as an impersonal, passive coercion only invites such terrifying outbreaks of police rioting. I am convinced, therefore, that no officer of "law and order" can preserve his decency under these conditions, where he is supposed to be a passive "instrument" of justice, a justice machine.

But in a dense city where power has been changed so that people are forced to deal directly with each other as men, not as parts of a planned order, aggressive hostilities involved in conflict could be directed to the objects of provocation. We are so enslaved to cowardly ideas of safety that we imagine direct expression of hostilities can only lead to brutal outbreaks. But such experiments in direct confrontation as the psychiatric "attack" sessions of Synanon games, where people are encouraged to express their hostile feelings about each other, almost never lead to blows, for the simple reason that there is no need for it. Hostility is actively expressed when felt, not left to fester and grow provoking.

It is said that American and western European cities are growing more violent. Some writers, like Oscar Handlin, doubt the historical validity of the assertion, and perhaps they are right to think that violent crime is no greater now than in the past. But the potential for "irrational crime," for violence without object or provocation, is very great now. The reason it exists is that society has come to expect too much order, too much coherence in its communal life, thus bottling up the hostile aggressiveness men cannot help but feeling.

These new anarchic cities promise to provide an outlet for what men now fear to show directly. In so doing, the structure of the city community will take on a kind of stability, a mode of ongoing expression, that will be sustaining to men because it offers them expressive outlets. Anarchy in cities, pushing men to say what they think about each other in order to forge some mutual patterns of compatability, is thus not a compromise between order and violence; it is a wholly different way of living, meaning that people will no longer be caught between these two polarities.

Why Men Will Want the New Cities

We have examined, thus far, why it would be good for the health of society if the cities of our times were changed, and why such good cities might be viable over time. But there remains an unanswered question in such a change: why should men *want* to make over their lives and inhabit these difficult cities? It is a question of convincing

men who have succeeded quite well in isolating themselves in warm and comforting shelters in the suburbs, or
in ethnic, racial, or class isolation, that these refuges are
worth abandoning for the terrors of the struggle to survive
together.

In exploring such personal desires, an urban study like
this is invading what was once the domain of moral
philosophers and theologians. Indeed, social studies are
now attempting definitions of the good and bad goals of
a life, the desirable forms of identity. Society has passed
beyond the stage where it sought from divine authority
firm and immutable answers to such questions, but the
questions remain, in all their messiness and refusal to
submit to the scalpel of numbers and quantitative answers: why should men want to lead a better communal
life than the comfortable one they now lead?

The immediate answer to this problem might seem that
these new cities would make a more just, compassionate
social order, and so in the end men would come to desire
them. This has been a great motive for belief in the Chris-
tian sects—i.e., that one can come to desire a good end
one has not yet experienced—but this belief is, I believe,
a great illusion as well. If men were saintly enough to
respond to such a plea, then the problems of untruthful-
ness and selfishness would never have arisen in the first
place. Indeed, these complex, overwhelming cities would
not really lead to a *self-conscious* awareness of being a
good person.

An anarchic survival community would not produce in
each man a knowledge that he is caring or learning to
care: he learns to care in order to survive, not in order to

be good. Such a break constitutes one divide between the ethics of our own time and the religious ethics of the past. Instead of advocating the practice of goodness for its own sake, which has, as Weber believed, come to such self-righteous and intolerant ends, a modern system of ethics must make an ethical condition emerge from social situations that are not consciously understood by the actors to be a search for a "better" ethical state. Looking for ethical situations in the structure of society is more honest, to my mind, than making pleas for a change of heart, more genuine than a conversion experience in which each man resolves to be good for ever after. People are too frail, and acts of mercy too easily perverted.

In his later novels, Dostoevsky gave another reason for looking at ethical desires in this way. He went so far as to believe a man could not be a good person if he were conscious of performing good acts; Dostoevsky felt that generosity and spontaneous giving become, when they reach a level of self-consciousness, a smug form of self-denial. Yet all the truly good figures in his later novels—Prince Mishkin, Alyosha, Maria—fail to survive; they are torn apart by their own goodness, because they have no other force animating their lives. These truly good men are beings without a consciousness of themselves, and with a total consciousness of others, so that they are destroyed by the very complexities of the people around them, into which they become enmeshed.

But the fate of such figures could be changed in the real world we could create in cities. In these cities, men will need to have some consciousness of themselves, they will continually be asking what it is in them that fails to be adequate for the social world they live in, what parts of their own lives are reconcilable or irreconcilable with the lives of the people around them. They cannot be unconsciousness of themselves if they are to survive; yet, like the good figures Dostoevsky pictured, they will be not conscious that what they do is good. For men struggling to understand each other in order to survive, the question of goodness would be irrelevant.

For example, we could imagine the everyday situation in which a man refuses to face the fact that a store he is building in a certain place in a neighborhood will eliminate a vacant lot children have needed to play in. The businessman is obdurate, and thus the neighbors, who are the only force to curb him in the absence of any central control, must begin a long process of threatening, cajoling, and harrassing so that they finally make him relent and look for a more socially acceptable site for his store. But applying this pressure—organizing boycotts and picket lines, etc.—is hardly a nourishing, satisfying task for most of the men involved in this new city role; the fact that they do something good for the community doesn't mean they like the substantive business of arguing with someone who regressed by willfully ignoring the people around him. It is the essence of a good act, as Dostoevsky said, that it does not bring a person pleasure to have been good.

How then can men become willing to endure the painful processes of a more civilized order? The force driving men into this new situation is, I believe, a specifically modern kind of boredom.

The people who in the last decade have searched in

their minds or activities for a new sense of "community" were products of the affluent suburbs for the most part. Their attitude toward these places where they grew up was strong and simple: the suburbs were boring, they were empty of life or surprise, and so on. The complaints are familiar to the point of becoming clichés. What is important about them is that a large segment of the present generation means to act according to their disenchantment with a boring past, and try to find something better. A sense of resignation is absent in these young people; they want actively to bring something new into being.

Part of this search for a new community is seen in the areas where young people are living and want to live. It has been known for some time that some of their parents, suburbanites whose children have grown up and left home, have been moving in increasing numbers back into the center of cities, when the housing is available. But an equally significant movement of young people into the center of cities is occurring. A growing minority of young adults, as they acquire family responsibilities and children, are refusing to make the trek out to the suburbs, and are searching instead for ways to remain in the center of town. The reason for this is that they hope for something "richer" in social life than what the suburb offers. It is true that a majority of the young married adults of this generation are moving into suburban homes of their own, just as the previous generation did. Yet among the more active, vital minority, a minority much greater than that to be found in the past, the old pattern is being rejected. These young people are refusing to be bored, refusing to accept the dead security in which they grew up.

It is my hope that this active refusal to accept the simplicities of the past will make it feasible for complex, disordered settlements to be desired and accepted by this generation nurtured in affluence. What someone has called the "great refusal" of the present generation to accept the secure cocoons the parents have woven can be the reason men now would be willing to endure the disorder and possible dislocation of an anarchic city environment.

This boredom is, however, rather strange. Most animals live by instinctual routines quite well; few men in agricultural, pre-industrial walks of life suffered from boredom, although their lives were hard and the rhythms of life fixed. The peculiar character of a secure, affluent routine is that it does not arise from the needs of adaptive survival with the environment or with other members of the race. It arises instead out of the fact that affluence permits men, through coherent routines, to hide from dealing with each other. Rather than face the full range of social experience possible to men, the communities of safe coherence cut off the amount of human material permitted into a man's life, in order that no questions of discord, no issues of survival be raised at all.

It is this "escape from freedom," in Erich Fromm's words, that ultimately makes a man quite consciously bored, aware that he is suffocating, although he may refuse to face the reasons for his suffocation. The boredom that rises out of this hiding is quite natural, for it is, as Nietzsche said, the voice of the creature in each man trying to make itself heard.

If social situations can be moved, step by step, toward

a social environment in which human diversity is permitted to express itself, I believe this "creature in the man" will take hold and become involved, driven by the boredom with what men do unnecessarily to keep themselves secure. The feeling of boredom in the new middle-class generation is the hidden, and, as yet, undeveloped expression of a desire for diversity. Once this hidden desire has a field in which to express itself, once cities become responsive to human needs, the tiredness with routine that men now experience will be the conscious force moving people step by step into encountering social diversity. Inevitably the question of how differences between men can coexist will then arise, and the men involved will be caught up in the process of urban growth such as I envision it.

The refusal of the young who have grown up in affluence to accept its routines as reality is a distinct emotional break with the traditional acceptance of routine under conditions of scarcity or deprivation. For the routinizing act has a real dignity when times are hard, and a refusal to accept routine seems to be the expression of a spoiled child. But that temper does not fit well the processes of a large segment of modern-day society. The routines of affluence seem, and are, *unnecessary*; there is no need for them when people have an adequate economic base. If there is any truth to the journalistic cries about the generation gap, it is that the old do not understand youth's perception of present reality and that they forget that the young have never known the corrosive power of scarcity, scarcity that drove their elders to see comfort and security as humanly dignified ends in a life.

Because of the great freedom for expressing conflict that affluence could bring, because of the possibility for satisfying men's desires to aggress against each other without the result of mutual destruction, because the routines of hiding produced by the present communal uses of affluence are proving so distasteful to those nurtured in them, I have dared to hope that the anarchic city might be more than a utopian dream, that it might be a viable alternative for what now passes as social life. Our affluence in its present form is becoming an intolerable weight to those who supposedly enjoy it. That is to say—beyond the fact that in much of western Europe and America affluence is so inequitably distributed—that even those who have it have not learned to use it for humane ends. Unlike Marcuse, I am convinced that affluence can be put to good ends, in a viable, enduring, anarchic society. I believe that the disgust and anxiety affluent communities presently cause in their young will make the people of this generation ready to explore the human unknown, and perhaps permit themselves to be hurt for the sake of preserving their vitality.

CHAPTER EIGHT

Conclusion: Ordinary Lives in Disorder

THIS BOOK CONTRASTS A SOCIETY THAT IS WITH A SOCIETY that could be. On the one hand, there exists a life in which the institutions of the affluent city are used to lock men into adolescence even when physically adult. On the other hand, there is the possibility that affluence and the structures of a dense, disorganized city could encourage men to become more sensitive to each other as they become fully grown. I believe the society that could be is not a utopian ideal; it is a better arrangement of social materials, which as organized today are suffocating people.

Yet the feel, the quality, of a social change is difficult to envision. People have only the sense of what they already have experienced, and that makes talk of social change seem abstract and unreal. To convey an impression of how these anarchic cities would affect ordinary life and everyday problems seems to me a fitting way to close this book.

Let us try to imagine what it would be like for one intelligent young girl who grows up in an anarchic urban milieu. She lives, perhaps, on a city square, with restaurants and stores mixed among the homes of her neighbors. When she and the other children go out to play, they do not go to clean and empty lawns; they go into the midst of people who are working, shopping, or are in the neighborhood for other reasons that have nothing to do with her. Her parents, too, are involved with their neighbors in ways that do not directly center on her and the other children of the neighborhood. There are neighborhood meetings where disruptive issues, like a noisy bar people want controlled, have to be fought out. Since the neighborhood is a densely packed place, thus permitting personal styles or deviations to be expressed, and since the personnel of the neighborhood is constantly shifting, her parents are out a great deal merely to find out who their neighbors are and see what kind of accommodations can be reached where conflicts arise. A black couple down the street may feel the little girl is cruel to their children, or some days she may feel they are cruel to her; the families cannot ignore each other. They are physically thrown together without impersonal resources, like attendance at homogeneous school districts, for separation.

In fact, the schools of the neighborhood are a kind of focus of conflict and conciliation for the parents. They are controlled by the community, but the community is so diverse that the schools cannot be pushed in any one direction. Families of the school district may have the right to set moral and religious policy for the school, for example, but since in these cities Catholics, Protestants, and Jews are mixed together, accommodations concerning ethical instruction and Bible training have to be arrived at. Indeed, the rules of the school shift constantly as new people in the district, with special backgrounds and interests, assert their right to have a hand in the shaping of their children's education.

But this little girl sees, every day, that the tensions and friendships in the community or school, so transitory and unstable, do not create chaos. She is made conscious of a kind of equilibrium of disorder in the lives of adults around her and in her own circle of friends. People are not sheltered from each other, but their contacts are more explorations of a constantly shifting environment than an acting out of unchanging routines.

Therefore this little girl grows up in a neighborhood that does not permit her family or her circle of friends to be intensive and inward-turning. This fact has a liberating power for her as someone who is exceptionally bright. For at school, the complex weave of friendship and casual acquaintance makes it very difficult for the other children to exercise pressure against her for being "different" because she is bright. In the suburbs, where social and economic backgrounds are ironed out, that pressure frequently and, in terms of the development of children like this, tragically arises. But in the city school this little girl attends, everyone is in some way different; there is a jumble of many backgrounds, and it becomes harder to shame someone who is unusual. Were this little girl exceptionally unintelligent, the same would be true. The children do not play and learn in packs; their backgrounds and their social contacts are too complex and too shifting for the brutal baiting that suburban children practice against kids who are "different" to work.

Let us now take a glimpse of this intelligent young girl later in her life, when she is a woman. Sociologists know something of what lies ahead for her in city culture as it exists now. Beyond all the clichés—made clichés by being so often true—of the inequities she will find in her work and the fear intelligent men show of treating her as an equal, her city life as an adult is today constricted in several less obvious ways. The forums for being with men as friends are usually limited to work; it is difficult outside this sphere to get to know people who aren't also after her. If and when she marries, there is usually an enormous amount of guilt about giving up her work and becoming just a housewife, since housewifely tasks, including her relations with other people in the community where she lives, offer little scope for exercising her intelligence. From what is known of young women like this, her life in a city faces two equally unacceptable alternatives of isolation: either a professional life where the opportunities of social encounters are limited to colleagues who feel competitive and men who want possession, or the more usual housewifely and community routines, which offer no field for intellect. But in a city where men and women are forced into all sorts of contact for accommodation and mutual survival, these poles of isolation can be greatly diminished. A single woman's work wouldn't define the sole society of peers in which she had to exist. It would be possible to meet a great number of people, in a variety of situations of mutual interest and curiosity, out of the necessity of dealing with her home neighborhood, her work neighborhood, and the city-wide political and social problems. Working in voluntary organizations or political clubs wouldn't be something an intelligent girl forced herself to do in order to meet men, as so often now occurs. These skeins of association would be a natural social life that arose out of the necessity for common action. Were a woman such as this to marry, have children and leave off her career, the same skein of necessary community relations would offer her a field to use her talents in ways that mattered. It is a commonplace that large numbers of middle-aged, intelligent housewives are left in suburbs with the time and desire to work in the communities where they live, but little room is given them in which to work, save as helpers or assistants to "real" professionals in schools or hospitals. By increasing the complexity and loosening the rules of routine in the community settings of these women, they would have a chance to be creative and have a forceful social life, even though they had opted out of professional careers.

A change in the kind of communities intelligent women can live in will not obviously change the whole complex of discrimination and fearfulness with which intelligent men and other women regard them. But for a young woman like the one I have described, the opprobrium of being different would be muted in childhood and adolescence; in adulthood the new anarchic communities would offer a means out of isolation whether the woman pursued a career or not.

Let us then try to envision the impact of anarchic cities on an ordinary group of city men: people from the "working class" who have become relatively affluent. A popular stereotype has it that such affluent industrial laborers and service personnel have become conservative and a force for the maintenance of repressive "law and order." It might seem, then, that they would be most resistant to social changes that introduced greater disorder into the city.

What researchers are beginning to glimpse about affluent working-class communities is that the cries for law and order are greatest when the communities are most isolated from other people in the city. In Boston, for example, the fear of deviance and conflict is much greater in an Irish area called South Boston, which is cut off geographically from contact with the city at large, than in another Irish area, North Cambridge, which is stuck in the midst of the city and is to some extent penetrated by blacks and college students. Cities in America during the past two decades have grown in such a way that ethnic areas have become relatively homogeneous; it appears no accident that the fear of the outsider has also grown to the extent that these ethnic communities have been cut off.

If the permeability of cities' neighborhoods were increased, through zoning changes and the need to share power across comfortable ethnic lines, I believe that working-class families would become more comfortable with people unlike themselves. The cries for law and order are enormously more complicated than the effect of community setting, and no one can pretend that a different kind of neighborhood would of itself transform the feelings of status insecurity or frustration in work that are involved in the desire for law and order. But the experience of living within diverse groups has its power. The enemies lose their clear image, because every day one sees so many people who are alien but who are not all alien in the same way.

Let us imagine a family where the father is an industrial worker moving into a disorganized community that forced family members into contact with others, with black families becoming affluent themselves, with managerial and professional people, with the young as well as the middle-aged. The image and demands of the neighborhood would work against whatever desire this family had for exclusion of the immoral, unpatriotic "them." But these communities would have a further, positive value to such a family as well.

In a community like this, the bureaucratic manipulation of conflict is gone. A factory man can confront those around him on a more equal basis than in a situation where middle-class bureaucracies prevail. The reason is that the willingness to use impersonal bureaucracy and faceless power has become the great weapon of the middle classes today over those who do routine labor. This weapon is purposely made weak in anarchic cities. It is patterns of personal influence and personal alliance that shape the balance of disorder in the new cities; politics and less formal community relations on these terms are historically how working-class people have evolved institu-

tions in which they feel a stake. I am convinced that in
such a milieu a man who does humble work can feel more
of a man in dealing with others than in circumstances
where the present weapons of power prevail. He can use
himself as a human being, make himself heard, rather
than be muffled by those who are different and more
skilled in the arts of bureaucratic management. Instead
of establishing common dignity by ensuring the sameness
of all who live in a community, as happens in so many affluent working-class areas now, this laboring family could
establish its dignity in a more satisfying way, by having a
community forum for conflict and reconciliation in which
it faces other people as concrete beings who have to talk
with each other.

In this way, a disordered city that forced men to deal
with each other would work to tone down feelings of
shame about status and helplessness in the face of large
bureaucracies. Participation of this sort could mute in
affluent workers that sad desire for repressive law and
order.

The final effect of the anarchic cities on the feelings of
ordinary people facing day-to-day problems concerns the
functional efficiency of the city itself. There is a Homeric
catalogue of complaints today about the quality of the
services and the environmental health of cities. Transportation is jammed, the air is polluted, the streets are
dirty; inadequate fire, police, and sanitation staffs strike
for more pay from cities that already operate at a loss;
most city schools are out of date and poorly equipped,
with inadequate provisions for teachers and staff.

These problems depend on more money, and this book

purposely provides no answers about new ways to make more tax dollars. Getting more money for cities in America is a brutally simple affair: the priorities of the economy have to be changed from massive military spending to a more just distribution of public resources. In the face of the military dominance of public finance, all other revenue-raising operations are "Bandaids," publicity devices that will have little real effect. The American economy is certainly able to finance the cities; after all, much less affluent countries whose budgets are not all-absorbed in military affairs have maintained their massive cities much more adequately than has the United States. As urbanists like myself have said over and over during the last few years, the urban financial problem in this country is the problem of military spending. Converting the economy from a military-industrial to an urban-industrial base is the only real solution.

But once the money is available, what is the best social use to which it can be put? As I have tried to show in this book, many of the seemingly routine aspects of city administration, like police, housing construction, and school administration, need not be routines, but opportunities for community life, thereby revitalizing the people directly concerned. Furthermore, I have sought to illustrate how the peculiar model of routing that has guided the planning of these services—a model based on the way machines produce goods—becomes dysfunctional and, in the words of the economists, counterproductive, when applied to the management of the social affairs of city men. Once the financial base for city services is expanded by a reduction in expenses for war, these services could become more responsive to the desires of city dwellers, if men could only accustom themselves to look at conflict over city services as a necessary, desirable product of people seeking to govern themselves. The social breakdown of city services—a strike by teachers, a strike by hospital staffs, etc.—is not an immoral threat to the public; these strikes are expressions of human need, voiced by people who want to be heard and are now thwarted by the central bureaucracies. Take conflict in the public arena away, and you revert to the idea that a broad swatch of urban society can have its best interests "managed" for it by impersonal bureaucratic means. As has been shown, this godlike presumption about other people's lives on the part of planners only builds up steam for violent disruption.

When conflict is permitted in the public sphere, when the bureaucratic routines become socialized, the product of the disorder will be a greater sensitivity in public life to the problems of connecting public services to the urban clientele. The financial crisis in city services caused by militarism has only served to reinforce the idea that "good" public service is one in which some measure of routine can function. Once the cash is available, the threats to routine will take on an entirely new character. The threats will be a focus of "sensitizing" public service bureaucracies to the public and to the public issues.

The fruit of this conflict—a paradox which is the essence of this book—is that in extricating the city from preplanned control, men will become more in control of themselves and more aware of each other. That is the promise, and the justification, of disorder.